THE **PASSION** TRANSLATION

1 & 2 Corinthians

LOVE
AND
TRUTH

Translated from Greek and Aramaic Texts

DR. BRIAN SIMMONS

tPt BIBLE

BroadStreet
PUBLISHING

1 & 2 Corinthians: Love and Truth, The Passion Translation®

Translated from the Greek and Aramaic texts by Dr. Brian Simmons

Published by BroadStreet Publishing Group, LLC
Racine, Wisconsin, USA
BroadStreetPublishing.com

© 2017 The Passion Translation®

ISBN-13: 978-1-4245-5174-3 (paperback)
ISBN-13: 978-1-4245-5175-0 (e-book)

Cover and design by Garborg Design Works, Inc. at garborgdesign.com
Typesetting by Katherine Lloyd at theDESKonline.com

Printed in the United States of America
17 18 19 20 5 4 3 2

1 Corinthians

Translator's Introduction to 1 Corinthians

AT A GLANCE

Author: The Apostle Paul

Audience: The Church of Corinth

Date: AD 53–55

Type of Literature: A letter

Major Themes: The gospel, the church, spiritual gifts, holiness, love, and the resurrection

Outline:

Letter Opening — 1:1–9
Causes and Cures of Division — 1:10–4:21
Moral Issues and Marriage — 5:1–7:40
Condemnation of Idolatry — 8:1–11:1
Affirmation of Worship and Gifts — 11:2–14:40
The Resurrection of the Dead — 15:1–58
Letter Closing — 16:1–24

ABOUT 1 CORINTHIANS

The once influential seaport city of Corinth was strategically located at the crossroads of the world. Prosperous, powerful, and decadent, it was a city that God wanted to reach with the power of the gospel. God sent the apostle Paul to Corinth on his third missionary journey to establish a church in a city that desperately needed love and truth. Paul spent a year and a half in Corinth and saw the church grow, with more believers being added to their number daily. But they needed wisdom from their spiritual father, Paul. So he wrote this letter to encourage them to carry on in their faith and to remain steadfast to the truths of the gospel.

Written while Paul was in Ephesus, this letter had a powerful effect on the Corinthian believers. In his second letter to them, he was able to take them even further into the truths of our new covenant reality and the power of the gospel to overcome sufferings. While Paul was ministering in Corinth, he met two people who would become his coworkers: Aquila and Priscilla, a husband-and-wife team.

Perhaps this book is best remembered for the so-called love chapter. In 1 Corinthians 13 we have the clearest and most poetic masterpiece of love in the New Testament. God's unending love always sustains us and gives us hope. Think how many of the problems in your life could be solved by embracing the revelation of love found in this anointed letter of Paul! May the love of God win every battle in your heart, bringing a full restoration of your soul into the image of God, for God is love.

We are so enriched by having this inspired letter, written to Paul's spiritual sons and daughters. How grateful we are that God has given us the treasures found in 1 Corinthians!

PURPOSE

Many see 1 Corinthians as a letter of correction. Indeed, many errors had crept into the belief system of the church of Corinth and the spiritual walk of its members. Some of the issues Paul needed to address include: living godly in a corrupt culture, being unified as one body without competition, maintaining the priority of sexual and moral purity within the church, understanding more completely the role of spiritual gifts in the context of the church, embracing love as the greatest virtue that must live within our hearts, maintaining orderly worship with proper respect toward one another, and keeping the hope of the resurrection burning brightly in our hearts.

But 1 Corinthians is not all correction. Paul gave many wonderful teachings to the young church that will impact your life as well. Like the Corinthian believers, you possess every spiritual gift, you are fully equipped to minister to others, you are capable of demonstrating love to all, and the hope of a future resurrection brings meaning to your life today.

AUTHOR AND AUDIENCE

The apostle Paul wrote to the church of Corinth not as an outsider but as one who was intimately involved in their affairs as a founding father (see Acts 18). He composed this letter about AD 53–55, while living in Ephesus. He was responding to certain issues and problems in the Corinthian church. Apparently, a delegation had arrived from Corinth and notified Paul of what was taking place and asked for his advice. First Corinthians was his response.

While this letter was directed to a specific congregation in a specific Roman city, we are as much of the audience today, given how we mirror many of the characteristics that defined Corinth. It was considered a modern, cosmopolitan city; its people were staunch individualists; their behaviors reflected this individualism; their spirituality was polytheistic; and believers accommodated the gospel in ways that made it palatable to the surrounding culture. These characteristics could also be said of us.

Corinth was the New York, London, and Sydney of the ancient world.

We need the voice of Paul and the Spirit of God to speak into our lives today. May we hear them clearly.

MAJOR THEMES

The Nature of the Gospel. This letter is gospel drenched! Not only in what it reveals about our story in Christ, but in what it reveals about his story too. In 8:6 we find revelation truth about Christ that hadn't been understood before: "For us there is only one God—the Father! He is the source of all things, and our lives are lived for him. There is one Lord, Jesus the Anointed One, through whom we, and all things, exist." Here Paul equates the one true God of Israel, Yahweh, with Jesus. Jesus is Yahweh, the only true God.

Paul also revealed the nature of our story, the story each of us has committed to by believing the gospel. Paul shared the core message that had been part of the church from the beginning: "The Messiah died for our sins. ... He was buried in a tomb and was raised from the dead after three days, as foretold in the Scriptures. Then he appeared to Peter the Rock and to the twelve apostles" (15:3–5). This is the essence of the gospel, the good news about our forgiveness from sins, freedom from shame and guilt, and new life in Christ. Like Paul, God's amazing grace found in this story has made us who we are.

The Church of Christ. One of the central issues Paul addressed was what we call ecclesiology, the nature of the church. What does it mean to be the people of God? What does it mean to gather as God's holy people—in Corinth, throughout America, or in Australia? One commentator declares these teachings on the church to be this letter's greatest theological contribution. As a church planter this makes sense. Paul was deeply concerned for his spiritual children and how they publicly professed and lived out the gospel in gathered community.

In this anointed letter, Paul confronted the nature of church leadership and pastoral ministry. He addressed lawsuits that were tearing believers apart. He confronted head-on the toleration of sexual immorality within the community. And he addressed the nature of worship, particularly the expression of God's supernatural gifts that God has imparted to every believer. No stone is left unturned as Paul shapes our understanding of what it means to be "God's inner sanctuary" (3:16); literally, "the body of Christ" (10:16) living and breathing in the world!

Holy and Ethical Living. In two of his other letters, Romans and Galatians, Paul made it clear that we are saved by grace through faith. In this letter, he makes it equally clear that we are "God's expensive purchase, paid for with tears of blood," and in response are called to "use your body to bring glory to God" (6:20). We do this by "following God's commandments" (7:19) and obeying "the law of Christ" (9:21).

No aspect of our new Christian ethics and holy living is left unaddressed. "People who continue to engage in sexual immorality, idolatry, adultery, sexual perversion, homosexuality, frauds, greed, drunkenness, verbal abuse, or extortion—these will not inherit God's kingdom realm" (6:9–10). We may be saved by grace, but Paul makes it clear that as Christians we are to live our lives in a way that glorifies and honors God (10:31).

Love, the Motivation of Our Lives. Each of Paul's letters seems to have an ethical high note. In his second letter to the Corinthians, it was generosity. In Ephesians, one could say it's humility. And Galatians emphasizes the fruit produced by the Spirit life. In this letter Paul uncovers the beautiful ethical prize after which we are to run: love. The so-called love chapter expounds upon the virtues of loving both God and neighbor, as Christ commanded. According to Paul, love is more worthy than speaking eloquently "in the heavenly tongues of angels" (13:1), better than having "unending supernatural knowledge" (13:2), far more important than giving away everything to the poor (13:3). As Paul says, "Love never stops loving"; it never fails (13:8).

Issues of "the End." By "the end" we mean both our personal end at death and also our world's end when Christ returns. While we often think our end hope is in heaven, it isn't. Our ultimate Christian hope is in the resurrection. Paul spent fifty-eight verses and an entire chapter making this clear. In fact, this was his main message. Jesus' resurrection from the dead paved the way for our own resurrection. He is "the first fruit of a great resurrection harvest of those who have died" (15:20). Because Jesus is alive, we have a bright hope for tomorrow. For this reason we can confidently declare, along with Paul, "Death is swallowed up by a triumphant victory! So death, tell me, where is your victory? Tell me, death, where is your sting?" (15:54–55).

A WORD ABOUT THE PASSION TRANSLATION

The message of God's story is timeless; the Word of God doesn't change. While the methods by which that story is communicated should be timely, the vessels that steward God's Word can and should change.

One of those timely methods and vessels is Bible translation. Bible translations are both a gift and a problem. They give us the words God spoke through his servants, but words can become poor containers for revelation because they leak! Words change from one generation to the next. Meaning is influenced by culture, background, and many other details.

There is no such thing as a truly literal translation of the Bible, for there is not an equivalent language that perfectly conveys the meaning of the biblical text as it was understood in its original cultural and linguistic setting. Therefore, translation can be a problem. The problem, however, is solved when we seek to transfer meaning, not merely words, from the original text to the receptor language.

The Passion Translation is a groundbreaking attempt to reintroduce the passion and fire of the Bible to the English reader. It doesn't merely convey the original, literal meaning of words. It expresses God's passion for people and his world by translating the original, life-changing message of God's Word for modern readers.

You will notice at times we've italicized certain words or phrases. These highlighted portions are not in the original Hebrew, Aramaic, and Greek manuscripts but are implied from the context. We've made these implications explicit for the sake of narrative clarity and to better convey the meaning of God's Word. This is a common practice used by mainstream translations, including the New American Standard Bible and the King James Version.

We've also chosen to translate certain names in their original Hebrew or Greek form to better convey their cultural meaning and significance. For instance, some translations of the Bible have substituted Miriam with Mary and Jacob with James. Both Greek and Aramaic leave the Hebrew names in their original form. Therefore, this translation uses their correct cultural names throughout.

God longs to have his Word expressed in every language in a way that would unlock the passion of his heart. Our goal is to trigger inside every English speaker an overwhelming response to the truth of the Bible. This is a heart-level translation, from the passion of God's heart to the passion of your heart.

We pray and trust this version of God's Word will kindle in you a burning, passionate desire for him and his heart, while impacting the church for years to come!

One

___

Paul's Greeting

[1]From Paul, divinely appointed according to the plan of God, to be an apostle of the Anointed One, Jesus. Our fellow believer Sosthenes[a] joins me [2]in writing you this letter addressed to the community of God[b] throughout the city of Corinth. For you have been made pure, set apart in the Anointed One, Jesus. And God has invited you to be his devoted and holy people, and not only you, but everyone everywhere who calls on the name of our Lord Jesus Christ as their Lord, and ours also.

[3]May joyous grace[c] and endless peace be yours continually from our Father God and from our Lord Jesus, the Anointed One!

Made Wonderfully Rich

[4]I am always thanking my God for you because he has given you such free and open access to his grace through your union with Jesus, the Messiah. [5]In him you have been made extravagantly rich in every way. You have been endowed with a wealth of inspired utterance[d] and the

---

a 1:1 Sosthenes means "savior of his nation." He was the Jewish synagogue ruler in Corinth who had converted to Christ and had been beaten for his faith (Acts 18:12–17).

b 1:2 Or "church." This is the Greek word *ekklēsia*, which means "a summoned people, called to assemble, a legislative body." It is also a word used in Greek culture to "assemble an army."

c 1:3 The Greek word *charis*, in its original sense, is descriptive of that which brings pleasure and joy to the human heart, implying a strong emotional element. God's grace includes favor and supernatural potency, and it is meant to leave us both charming and beautiful. In classical Greek it was meant to convey the attitude of favor shown by royalty. See Torrance, *The Doctrine of Grace in the Apostolic Fathers*, pp. 1–5.

d 1:5 Or "in every kind of speaking." By implication, Paul is commending them for their speaking gifts (prophecy, tongues and interpretation of tongues, preaching, and teaching the word of God). This will be developed further in chapters 12–14.

riches that come from your intimate knowledge of him. [6]For the reality of the truth of Christ is seen among you and strengthened[a] through your experience of him. [7]So now you aren't lacking any spiritual gift[b] as you eagerly await the unveiling[c] of the Lord Jesus, the Anointed One. [8]He will keep you steady and strong to the very end, making your character mature so that you will be found innocent on the day of our Lord Jesus Christ. [9]God is forever faithful and can be trusted to do this in you, for he has invited you to co-share the life of his Son,[d] Jesus, the Anointed One, our King![e]

Paul Addresses Divisions in the Church

[10]I urge you, my brothers and sisters, for the sake of the name of our Lord Jesus Christ, to agree to live in unity with one another[f] and put to rest any division that attempts to tear you apart.[g] Be restored[h] as one united

---

a 1:6 Or "validated" or "confirmed." The word used here is found in classical Greek in the context of establishing (building) communities.

b 1:7 Or "You don't fail to receive any gift of the Holy Spirit." God wants his church to receive every gift the Holy Spirit has to give us. This may be a figure of speech called a litotes, which means it could also be translated, "You have every spiritual gift."

c 1:7 Or "eagerly accept" or "eagerly await." The Greek word *ekdechomai* is a compound word, *ek* (out of, from) and *dechomai* (to accept or receive or take hold of).

d 1:9 Or "a life of communion with his Son." That is, a co-participation (communion, fellowship) of the Son. The Aramaic is "You have been called to the (wedding) feast of his Son." We see a clear picture here that believers are called to share in the sonship of Jesus. By God's grace, we will share in the Son's standing and position before the Father. We are not only blameless but made holy by the co-sharing of the life of God's Son.

e 1:9 Or "Lord."

f 1:10 Or "that you all speak the same thing"; that is, to have a united testimony. The Aramaic is "that you may all be of one word."

g 1:10 The congregation of believers in Corinth was sorely divided. They had divided over which leader or apostle they followed (chapters 1–3), over the limits of their freedom (chapters 6–8), over their socio-economic status (chapter 11), and over spiritual gifts (chapters 12–14). Division among believers grossly hinders our message and ministry to the world of unbelievers. Paul is pleading with them to unite around the love of God for one another (chapter 13).

h 1:10 Or "fully equipped."

body living in perfect harmony. Form a consistent choreography among yourselves, having a common perspective with shared values.

[11]My dear brothers and sisters, *I have a serious concern I need to bring up with you,*[a] for I have been informed by those of Chloe's *house church*[b] that you have been destructively arguing among yourselves. [12]And I need to bring this up because each of you is claiming loyalty to different preachers. Some are saying, "I am a disciple of Paul," or, "I follow Apollos," or, "I am a disciple of Peter the Rock,"[c] and some, "I belong *only* to Christ." [13]But *let me ask you,* is Christ divided up into groups? Did I die on the cross for you? At your baptism did you pledge yourselves to follow Paul?[d]

[14]Thank God I only baptized two from Corinth—Crispus and Gaius![e] [15]So now no one can say that in my name I baptized others.[f] [16](Yes, I also baptized Stephanus and his family. Other than that, I don't remember baptizing anyone else.) [17]For the Anointed One has sent me on a mission, not to see how many I could baptize,[g] but to proclaim the good

---

a 1:11 Before Paul brought correction to the Corinthians, he first affirmed the work of God in their midst. See 1 Corinthians 1:4–9. Perhaps we should look at confused and messed-up Christians differently and speak to how God sees imperfect believers.

b 1:11 Or "Chloe's people." The word *household* or *family* is not in the Greek text. By implication, it refers to those who are meeting with Chloe, as the one they are connected to (Chloe's people; i.e., house church, or Chloe's congregation). She was obviously a trusted leader in Paul's estimation and had influence in the church of Corinth. Her name means "green (tender) sprout." Those who informed Paul of the problems in Corinth may have been Stephanas, Fortunatus, and Achaicus, mentioned in 1 Corinthians 16:17.

c 1:12 Or "Cephas," the Aramaic word for rock (*keefa*) transliterated into Greek. Paul is comfortable in calling Peter by his Aramaic nickname, Keefa.

d 1:13 Or "Were you baptized in the name of Paul?"

e 1:15 Before converting to faith in Christ, Crispus was likely the ruler of the synagogue in Corinth mentioned in Acts 18:18. Gaius was most likely the one who hosted Paul when he came to Rome (Romans 16:23). Since they had become believers before Paul's assistants, Timothy and Silas, arrived from Macedonia, Paul went ahead and baptized them.

f 1:15 As translated from the Aramaic. The Greek is "so that no one can say that they were baptized in my name."

g 1:17 In the broader context of Paul's teaching, both baptism and the Lord's Table proclaim the Lord Jesus (Romans 6:3–11 and 1 Corinthians 11:24–27). Therefore, viewing

news. And I declare this message stripped of all philosophical arguments that empty the cross of its true power. For I trust in the all-sufficient cross of Christ alone.

The True Power of the Cross

[18]To preach the message[a] of the cross seems like sheer nonsense to those who are on their way to destruction, but to us who are on our way to salvation, it is the mighty power of God released within us.[b] [19]For it is written:

> I will dismantle the wisdom of the wise
> and I will invalidate the intelligence of the scholars.[c]

[20]So where is the wise philosopher *who understands?* Where is the expert scholar *who comprehends?* And where is the skilled debater of our time *who could win a debate with God?* Hasn't God demonstrated that the wisdom of this world system is utter foolishness?

[21]For in his wisdom, *God designed that all* the world's wisdom would be insufficient to lead people to the discovery of himself. He took great delight in baffling the wisdom of the world by using the simplicity of preaching the story of the cross[d] in order to save those who believe it. [22]For the Jews constantly demand to see miraculous signs, while those

---

Paul's statement as somewhat hyperbolic, it is taken to mean that he was not sent *just* to baptize but also *to preach* the gospel.

a 1:18 Or "expression (Greek, *logos*)" or "the act of proclaiming."

b 1:18 The *message of the cross* becomes the ignition point where God's power becomes operative and actualized with the ability to convert, transform, and save. The Aramaic can be translated "For he (rather than the message) is the power of God."

c 1:19 See Isaiah 29:14 LXX. Paul uses the prophecy of Isaiah as a warning against leaning upon human wisdom to understand spiritual matters. True wisdom comes from above and is given by divine revelation to those who are teachable and humble before God.

d 1:21 Or simply "the foolishness of preaching." However, it is not the act of preaching but the content of what is preached that brings salvation to those who believe.

who are not Jews[a] constantly cling to the world's wisdom,[b] 23but we preach the crucified Messiah. The Jews stumble over him and the rest of the world sees him as foolishness. 24But for those who have been chosen to follow him, both Jews and Greeks, he is God's mighty power, God's true wisdom, and our Messiah.[c] 25For the "foolish" things of God have proven to be wiser than human wisdom. And the "feeble" things of God have proven to be far more powerful than any human ability.[d]

God's Calling

26Brothers and sisters, consider who you were when God called you *to salvation*. Not many of you were wise scholars by human standards, nor were many of you in positions of power. Not many of you were considered the elite *when you answered God's call.* 27But God chose those whom the world considers foolish to shame those who think they are wise, and God chose the puny and powerless to shame[e] the high and mighty. 28He chose the lowly, the laughable[f] in the world's eyes—nobodies—so that he would shame the somebodies. For he chose what is regarded as insignificant in order to supersede what is regarded as

---

a 1:22 The Aramaic uses the term Arameans for Gentiles. It means "Aramaic-speaking people."

b 1:22 To paraphrase, the Gentiles seek for success in the world's eyes, or a wisdom that leads them to succeed. Christ crucified is both a miracle sign and the wisdom that will lead one to reign in life.

c 1:24 Christ is the supreme manifestation of God's power to save us from sin, to work miracles, and to defeat evil. Christ is the supreme manifestation of wisdom, for he carries out the eternal plan of God and brings it to completion.

d 1:25 Although the cross seemed to be the foolishness of God, it reveals his transcendent wisdom. And though God the Son was crucified in weakness, he has risen through the divine power that transforms lives today. God has no weakness or foolishness whatsoever. Yet what looks like weakness is actually his strength, and what looks like foolishness is actually his wisdom.

e 1:27 The Greek word *kataischynō* can also be translated "embarrass, confuse, baffle, or frustrate."

f 1:28 Or "despised, disgusting, outcasts, perceived with contempt."

prominent, [29]so that there would be no place for prideful boasting in God's presence. [30]*For it is not from man that we draw our life* but from God as we are being joined to Jesus, the Anointed One. And now he is our God-given wisdom, our virtue, our holiness, and our redemption. [31]And this fulfills what is written:

> **If anyone boasts, let him only boast**
> **In all that the Lord has done!**[a]

Two

Paul's Reliance on Spiritual Power

[1]My brothers and sisters,[b] when I first came to proclaim to you the secrets[c] of God, I refused to come *as an expert*, trying to impress you with my eloquent speech and lofty wisdom. [2]For while I was with you I was determined to be consumed with one topic—Jesus, the crucified Messiah.[d] [3]I stood before you feeling inadequate, filled with reverence

---

a 1:31 Or "He who triumphs, let him triumph in the Lord God!" See Jeremiah 9:24.

b 2:1 Or "brothers."

c 2:1 As translated from the Aramaic. Some Greek manuscripts have "testimony." Paul, as a steward of the mysteries of God (1 Corinthians 4:1), comes to them bringing a clear revelation of God's mysteries. The Greek word *mustērion* (secret, or mystery) is found twenty-eight times in the New Testament.

d 2:2 Paul could have easily impressed the Corinthians with his vast knowledge of the Torah and the Jewish laws. But he was resolved to forget every other topic and stay focused on Christ and his cross. He wanted the power of the Spirit to work through his singular message.

for God,[a] and trembling *under the sense of the importance of my words.*[b] [4]The message I preached and how I preached it was not an attempt to sway you with persuasive arguments but to prove to you the almighty power of God's Holy Spirit. [5]For God intended that your faith not be established on man's wisdom but by trusting in his almighty power.

Wisdom from God

[6]However, there is a wisdom that we continually speak of when we are among the spiritually mature.[c] It's wisdom that didn't originate in this present age, nor did it come from the rulers of this age who are in the process of being dethroned.[d] [7]Instead, we[e] continually speak of this wonderful wisdom that comes from God, hidden before now in a mystery.[f] It is his secret plan, destined[g] before the ages, *to bring* us into glory.[h] [8]None of the rulers of this present world order understood it,[i] for if they had,

---

a 2:3 As translated from the Aramaic. The Greek is "I was with you in fear and trembling."

b 2:3 Paul was not simply filled with dread or fear, but filled with how important it was to present the gospel clearly to the Corinthians. See also 2 Corinthians 10:10 and 11:6.

c 2:6 Or "those who have reached perfection." The Greek term for *spiritually mature* in this verse is found in classical Greek, describing those who have been *initiated into mysteries.* It most likely refers in this context to those who believed Paul's message containing the mysteries of God (2:1). Paul uses the word *wisdom* sixteen times in the first three chapters of 1 Corinthians.

d 2:6 Or "rulers who are doomed to come to nothing" or "the nullified overlords of this present age." This does not refer merely to human governments, but to the dethroned rulers of darkness that know nothing of God's secret wisdom.

e 2:7 Many times in 1 and 2 Corinthians when Paul uses the pronoun *we,* he is referring to the apostles of the church, gifts of Christ who are sent to teach the mysteries of God. See Ephesians 4:11–13 and 1 Corinthians 4:1.

f 2:7 That is, something so profound it is beyond the scope of human ingenuity and unattainable by human reasoning. Wisdom comes from above and is given to those who love God and live in awe of him.

g 2:7 Or "decreed." The Greek word *proorizo* means "to mark out the boundaries." It is a form of the word *horizon.* God has marked out ahead of time the horizon of the ages and will finish his predetermined plan perfectly.

h 2:7 The Aramaic is "for our glorification" or "so that glory may be ours."

i 2:8 Although it is possible that this refers to human rulers, it is hard to imagine how Herod, Pilate, and the Jewish authorities could be equated to the words "rulers of (over)

they never would have crucified the Lord of Shining Glory.[a] [9]This is why the Scriptures say:

Things never discovered or heard of before,
things beyond our ability to imagine—[b]
these are the many things God has in store
for all his lovers.[c]

[10]But God now unveils these profound realities to us by the Spirit.[d] Yes, he has revealed to us his inmost heart and deepest mysteries through the Holy Spirit, who constantly explores all things. [11]After all, who can really see into a person's heart and know his hidden impulses except for that person's spirit. So it is with God. His thoughts and secrets are only fully understood by his Spirit, the Spirit of God.

[12]For we did not receive the spirit of this world system but the Spirit of God, so that we might come to understand and experience all that grace has lavished upon us. [13]And we[e] articulate these realities with the words imparted to us by the Spirit and not with the words taught by human wisdom. We join together Spirit-revealed truths with Spirit-revealed words.[f]

---

this present age (*aeon*)." It seems clear that Paul is speaking of the principalities and powers of darkness, who were clueless about the efficacy of Christ's crucifixion to realign the universe and initiate a new kingdom under our Lord Jesus Christ.

a 2:8 Or a genitive of quality, "the Lord, to whom glory belongs." This is the only place in the New Testament with the term "Lord of Glory." The church father Augustine translated this "the Lord who dispenses glory" (an objective genitive: Augustine, *On the Trinity*, 1:12:24).

b 2:9 Or "entered the heart."

c 2:9 See Isaiah 64:4.

d 2:10 Or "God has provided us with a revelation through the Spirit." This difficult-to-translate Greek sentence may contain an ellipsis, which would render it "Yet *we speak* (or *we know*) what God has revealed to us by the Spirit."

e 2:13 It is possible that Paul uses *we* in reference to apostles.

f 2:13 Or "We explain spiritual realities to spiritual people" or "We interpret spiritual truths by spiritual faculties."

[14]Someone living on an entirely human level[a] rejects[b] the revelations of God's Spirit, for they make no sense to him. He can't understand the revelations of the Spirit because they are only discovered by the illumination of the Spirit. [15]Those who live in the Spirit are able to carefully evaluate all things, and they are subject to the scrutiny of no one *but God.* [16]For

> **Who has ever intimately known the mind of the Lord Yahweh**[c]
> **well enough to become his counselor?**[d]

Christ has, and we possess Christ's perceptions.[e]

Three

A Call to Spiritual Maturity

[1]Brothers and sisters, when I was with you I found it impossible to speak to you as those who are spiritually mature people, for you are still dominated by the mind-set of the flesh. And because you are immature infants

---

a 2:14 Or "the natural man" or "the one without the Spirit." The Aramaic is "A man in his natural self cannot receive spiritual concepts."

b 2:14 Or "does not have access to."

c 2:16 As translated from the Aramaic.

d 2:16 See Isaiah 40:13.

e 2:16 That is, we believers possess the Holy Spirit, who reveals the thoughts and purposes of Christ. The revelation of the kingdom of God that Jesus preached was not understood by the intellect of men but by those who welcomed his truth. Humanly speaking, no one can understand the mysteries of God without the Holy Spirit. Those who have the Holy Spirit now possess the perceptions of Christ's mind and can implement his purposes on the earth.

in Christ, ²I had to nurse you and feed you with "milk,"ᵃ not with the solid food *of more advanced teachings*, because you weren't ready for it. In fact, you are still not ready to be fed solid food, ³for you are living your lives dominated by the mind-set of the flesh. Ask yourselves: Is there jealousy among you? Do you compare yourselves with others? Do you quarrel *like children* and end up taking sides? If so, this proves that you are living your lives centered on yourselves, dominated by the mind-set of the flesh, and behaving like unbelievers. ⁴For when you divide yourselves up in groups—a "Paul group" and an "Apollos group"ᵇ—you're acting like people without the Spirit's influence.ᶜ

⁵Who is Apollos, really? Or who is Paul? Aren't we both just servants through whom you believed our message? Aren't each of us doing the ministry the Lord has assigned to us? ⁶I was the one who planted the church and Apollos came and cared for it, but it was God who caused it to grow. ⁷This means the one who plants is not anybody special, nor the one who waters, for God is the one who brings the supernatural growth.

⁸Now, the one who plants and the one who waters are *equally import-ant* and on the same team, but each will be rewarded for his own work. ⁹We are coworkers with Godᵈ and you are God's cultivated garden, the house he is building. ¹⁰God has given me unique giftsᵉ as a skilled mas-

---

a 3:2 This "milk" would include the basic teachings of our faith. Even so, every newborn needs milk to survive and be sustained. See 1 Peter 2:2. The more advanced teachings Paul describes are spiritual "meat"—something we can "sink our teeth into" and look for deeper meaning in.

b 3:4 Apollos was a brilliant, educated Alexandrian Jew and a follower of John the Immerser. While in Ephesus, Apollos met Priscilla and Aquila, who directed him into deeper teachings of Christ (Acts 18:24–26). Apparently the church of Corinth was deeply divided and in need of wisdom and unity.

c 3:4 Or "Are you (merely) men?"

d 3:9 Workers have different gifts and abilities, but true growth of God's kingdom is through divine power. No one is a superstar; we are all members on God's team.

e 3:10 Or "grace (for the task)."

ter builder[a] who lays a good foundation. Afterward another craftsman comes and builds on it. So builders beware! Let every builder do his work carefully, according to God's standards. [11]For no one is empowered to lay an alternative foundation other than the good foundation that exists, which is Jesus Christ!

[12-13]The quality of materials used by anyone building on this foundation will soon be made apparent, whether it has been built with gold, silver, and costly stones,[b] or wood, hay, and straw. Their work will soon become evident, for the Day[c] will make it clear, because it will be revealed by blazing fire! And the fire will test and prove the workmanship of each builder. [14]If his work stands the test of fire, he will be rewarded. [15]If his work is consumed by the fire, he will suffer great loss. Yet he himself will barely escape destruction, like one being rescued out of a burning house.

The Church, God's Inner Sanctuary

[16]Don't you realize that together you have become God's inner sanctuary[d]

---

a 3:10 Or "wise, first-class architect." We would say in today's English, "a top-notch general contractor."

b 3:15 Paul's language seems to be anticipating his next subject: the church as God's true temple. There is here an allusion to the temple of Solomon, which was built using gold, silver, and costly stones. Wisdom will build her house with divine substance (gold), redemption's fruit (silver), and transformed lives (costly stones). See 1 Chronicles 22:14–16 and 29:2. Wood, hay, and straw are emblems of the works of the flesh, the building materials of men, not of God. They grow up from the ground, which God cursed (Genesis 3:17). It is both quality and durability that God commends. Fire will cause the better material to glow brighter, but the inferior material will be consumed. How we build and what we build matters to God. Note that it is possible to build on the true foundation of Christ but with wrong materials. We need God's work done in God's way.

c See Romans 2:16; 1 Corinthians 1:8; 4:5; 5:5; 2 Corinthians 5:9–10; 2 Thessalonians 1:10.

d 3:16 Or "temple." The plural you (you all) shows that Paul is referring to the church, the body of believers, the holy dwelling place of God on earth. Later, in 1 Corinthians 6:19, he refers to individual believers (our human bodies) as the dwelling place of God. Ten times in 1 Corinthians Paul uses the phrase "Don't you know (realize)?"

and that the Spirit of God makes his permanent home in you?[a] [17]Now, if someone desecrates[b] God's inner sanctuary, God will desecrate him, for God's inner sanctuary is holy, and that is exactly who you are.

True Wisdom

[18]So why fool yourself and live under an illusion?[c] Make no mistake about it, if anyone thinks he is wise by the world's standards, he will be made wiser by being a fool for God![d] [19]For what the world says is wisdom is actually foolishness in God's eyes. As it is written:

> The cleverness of the know-it-alls
> becomes the trap[e] that ensnares them.

[20]And again:

> The Lord sees right through
> the clever reasonings of the wise
> and knows that it's all a sham.[f]

[21]So don't be proud of your allegiance to any human leader. For actually, you already have everything! It has all been given for your benefit, [22]whether it is Paul or Apollos or Peter the Rock,[g] or whether it's the

---

a 3:16 God revealed his presence in the Old Testament temple by filling it with a cloud of glory. The New Testament inner sanctuary is now the church, where God dwells among us by his Spirit.

b 3:17 Or "If someone destroys God's temple, God will destroy him." The Aramaic uses the word *deface* or *shatter*.

c 3:18 For every verse that warns us of being deceived by others, there is verse to warn us about being self-deceived. Having a teachable heart and learning wisdom from above is the best way to guard from self-deception.

d 3:18 As translated from the Aramaic. The Greek is "If anyone thinks he is wise by the world's standards, he must first become ignorant (or silly) and then he can become truly wise."

e 3:19 The Greek word *drassomai* means "to close the fist on" or, by implication, "to trap, or firmly grasp (a slippery object)." See Job 5:13.

f 3:20 See Psalm 94:11.

g 3:22 Or "Cephas," which is the Latin spelling of *keefa*, the Aramaic word for "rock." God

world[a] or life or death,[b] or whether it's the present or the future—everything belongs to you! 23And now you are joined to the Messiah, who is joined to God.

Four

Apostolic Ministry

1So then you must perceive us—*not as leaders of factions,* but as servants[c] of the Anointed One, those who have been entrusted[d] with God's mysteries. 2The most important quality of one entrusted with such secrets is that they are faithful and trustworthy. 3But personally, I'm not the least bit concerned if I'm judged by you or any verdict I receive from any human court. In fact, I don't even assume to be my own judge, 4even though my

---

places all of his servants at the disposal of the church. Leaders come and go, but God's work continues. Every gift and every leader is meant to serve the body of Christ and bring her into the fullness of Christ.

a 3:22 The Aramaic is "the universe." That is, the church is not of this world; it is to bring heaven's kingdom into the forefront of all the world. The wisdom of the world is subdued by God's wisdom given to the church.

b 3:22 That is, the pressures of life and death are beneath the rule of Christ in our hearts. See Romans 14:9. The days of our present life, as well as the future glory, belong to us already. We are not victims in life, for as believers we share in the lordship of Christ today and forever.

c 4:1 Paul uses an unusual Greek word, *huperetes,* which means "subordinate or personal assistant." The compound word *huperetes* literally means "under-rowers," and it is used in classical Greek to describe those who sit on benches in the lower parts of the ship rowing. Apostolic ministry does not mean that an apostle is seen as important and in first place, but as one who will often be in a hidden role of moving a church and region forward as a subordinate of our Captain, Jesus Christ.

d 4:1 Or "stewards (estate managers, trustees)." Paul is here referring to the apostles who helped establish and set in order the church at Corinth.

conscience is clear. But that doesn't mean I stand acquitted before the Lord,[a] for the only judge I care about is him!

⁵So resist the temptation to pronounce premature judgment on anything before the appointed time *when all will be fully revealed.* Instead, wait until the Lord makes his appearance, for he will bring all that is hidden in darkness to light[b] and unveil every secret motive of everyone's heart. Then, *when the whole truth is known,* each will receive praise from God.[c]

The Ministry of True Apostles

⁶Dear brothers and sisters, I've been referring allusively to myself and Apollos in order to illustrate what I've been saying. It is futile to move beyond what is written in the Scriptures and be inflated with self-importance by following and promoting one leader in competition with another. ⁷For what makes a distinction between you and someone else?[d] And what do you have that grace has not given you?[e] And if you received it *as a gift,* why do you boast as though there is something special about you?[f]

---

a 4:4 Both here and in verse 5, the Aramaic is "Lord Yahweh."

b 4:5 The Aramaic is "He will pour light upon the hidden things of darkness."

c 4:5 The clear inference is that God will bring to light the secret motives of love, faithfulness, righteousness, kindness, etc.—not only evil motives, but the pure motives of believers. When the Lord judges his godly lovers, their secret devotion and sacrifices will all be brought into the light and God will praise them for their faithful love. The reward of eternity will be that God affirms them. The word for "praise" can actually be translated, "thanks from God." Can you imagine the day coming when God praises his faithful servants? See also 1 John 4:17–19.

d 4:7 Or "Who sees anything different in you?" The answer to this rhetorical question is "God."

e 4:7 Or "What do you have that you have not received?" The answer to this rhetorical question is "Nothing."

f 4:7 Or "Why do you boast as though you did not (receive it because of grace)?" The church at Corinth was split into different factions, each following a different leader. Apparently, each clique thought they had the truth because they had a more anointed leader. But Paul exhorts them not to put their confidence in their hero-leader, because each leader is nothing more than a servant who receives God's grace to minister accord-

[8]Oh, I know, you already have all you need![a] Since when did you become so content and rich without us? You've already crowned yourselves as royalty, reigning on your thrones, leaving us *lowly apostles* far behind![b] How I wish indeed that you really were reigning as kings already, for that would mean we would be reigning as kings alongside of you.[c]

Apostolic Model of Ministry

[9]It seems to me that God has appointed us apostles to be at the end of the line. We are like those on display at the end of the procession, as doomed gladiators soon to be killed. We have become a theatrical spectacle to all creation, both to people and to angels. [10]We are fools for Christ, but you are wise in Christ! We are the frail; you are the powerful. You are celebrated;[d] we are humiliated. [11]If you could see us now, you'd find that we are hungry and thirsty, poorly clothed,[e] brutally treated,[f] and with no roof over our heads.[g] [12]We work hard, toiling with our own hands. When people abuse and insult us, we respond with a blessing,

---

ing to his or her gift. No leader has a greater status than another.

a 4:8 The Greek text uses a metaphor of overfed farmyard animals. They were stuffed with self-importance.

b 4:8 See Revelation 3:17. A smug, religious self-satisfaction is to have no place in our hearts. We must continually thirst for more of God. We have all things in Christ, but not all that He has given us has filled our hearts. Though we have every blessing, we must walk it out in our daily lives. With biting irony Paul uncovers their pride in thinking they have left the poor apostles behind and have become independent—greater and with more kingdom wealth than they. The deprivations and struggles of the apostles were looked down upon by the Corinthians. See also 2 Corinthians 11:12–12:1. Although verse 8 is in the form of posing rhetorical questions (irony), it is possible to translate it this way: "You have already become full (like at a feast) and fully satisfied. You are already suddenly rich. You suddenly reign as kings apart from us."

c 4:8 The Aramaic continues the irony. "Come, share your royal reign with us so we too can rule with you!"

d 4:10 Or "famous."

e 4:11 Or "wearing rags (tattered and threadbare)."

f 4:11 Or "brutally beaten (hit with fists)." See Matthew 26:67 and 2 Corinthians 11:26.

g 4:11 Or "homeless."

and when severely persecuted, we endure it with patience. [13]When we are slandered incessantly, we always answer gently,[a] ready to reconcile. Even now, in the world's opinion, we are nothing but filth[b] and the lowest scum.

A Father's Warning

[14]I'm not writing this to embarrass you or to shame you, but to correct you as the children I love. [15]For although you could have countless babysitters[c] in Christ *telling you what you're doing wrong*, you don't have many fathers *who correct you in love*. But I'm a true father to you, for I became your father when I gave you the gospel and brought you into union with Jesus, the Anointed One. [16]So I encourage you, my children, to follow the example that I live before you.[d]

[17]That's why I've sent my dear son Timothy, whom I love. He is faithful to the Lord Yahweh[e] and will remind you of how I conduct myself as one who lives in union with Jesus, the Anointed One, and of the teachings that I bring to every church everywhere.

[18]There are some among you who have exalted themselves as if I were not coming back to you. [19]But I will come soon, if it pleases the Lord, and I will find out not only what these arrogant ones are saying, but also if they have power to back up their words! [20]For the kingdom realm of God comes with power, not simply impressive words. [21]So which would you prefer? Shall I come carrying the rod of authority to discipline or with an embrace in love with a gentle spirit?

---

a 4:13 Or "We appeal to them (directly)."

b 4:13 Or "scapegoats."

c 4:15 Or "guardians (tutors)."

d 4:16 Or "Imitate me." The Aramaic is "I want you to resemble me." Paul is saying, "Prove your parentage by your conduct; follow me like a father."

e 4:17 As translated from the Aramaic. The Greek is "He is faithful (dependable) in the Lord."

Five

Immorality in the Church

[1-2]It's been widely reported that there is gross sexual immorality among you—the kind of immorality that's so revolting it's not even tolerated by the social norms of unbelievers.[a] Are you proud of the fact that one of your men is having sex with his stepmother?[b] Shouldn't this heartbreaking scandal bring you to your knees in tears? You must remove the offender from among you!

[3]Even though I am physically far away from you, my spirit is present with you. And as one who is present with you, I have already evaluated and judged the perpetrator. [4]So *call a meeting*, and when you gather together in the name of our Lord Jesus, and you know my spirit is present with you in the infinite power of our Lord Jesus,[c] [5]release this man over to Satan[d] for the destruction of his *rebellious* flesh, in hope that his spirit may be rescued and restored in the day of the Lord.[e]

---

a 5:1-2 Or "pagans (Gentiles)."

b 5:1-2 Or "his father's wife." This incestuous relationship was forbidden by the Law. See Leviticus 18:8. The sin is more than the illicit acts of this unnamed man, but the tolerance of a church that refused to correct and deal with the sin in their midst. Indeed, this chapter implies that the church was somewhat smug and arrogant ("puffed up") over conduct that violated sensibility.

c 5:4 God had given Paul exceptional ability to have his spirit present, along with the power of God, in their meetings together.

d 5:5 Satan means "accusing adversary." When one is put out of the fellowship of the church family, the Accuser has access to harass and oppress. There is a blessed protection in the fellowship of God's people, for the Lord is present with us when we gather in his name.

e 5:5 Or "Turn this man over to Satan for the destruction of your fleshly works so that your spirit may be saved in the day of the Lord." Verses 3 through 5 is one long, complicated Greek sentence. Many see this difficult passage as a prescription for ex-communication from the church. Aramaic speakers see in this passage the words "Turn him over to

⁶Boasting *over your tolerance of sin* is inappropriate. Don't you understand that even a small compromise with sin permeates the entire fellowship, just as a little leaven permeates a batch of dough? ⁷So remove every trace of your "leaven" of compromise with sin so that you might become new and pure again. For indeed, you are clean[a] because Christ, our Passover Lamb, has been sacrificed for us.[b] ⁸So now we can celebrate our continual feast, not with the old "leaven," the yeast of wickedness or bitterness, but we will feast on the freshly baked bread of innocence and holiness.[c]

Correcting a Misunderstanding

⁹I wrote you *in my previous letter*[d] asking you not to associate with those who practice sexual immorality.[e] ¹⁰Yet in no way was I referring to avoiding contact with unbelievers who are immoral, or greedy, or swindlers, or those who worship other gods—for that would mean you'd have to

---

the Accuser," as a figure of speech meaning "Let him suffer the consequences of his actions." We have similar sayings in English. "Let him stew in his own juices." Or "Give him enough rope to hang himself." Or "Let him learn his lesson the hard way." Regardless, it is not a light thing to be handed over to Satan. Apparently this man learned his lesson and repented, for Paul instructs the Corinthians in his second letter to forgive and comfort him. See 2 Corinthians 2:6–11.

a 5:7 Or "unleavened." Paul uses encouragement here to stir them to embrace a lifestyle that is already theirs. We are all made "clean" by the blood of the Lamb.

b 5:7 Verses 6 and 7 contain the interesting metaphor of yeast and its effect on a batch of dough. It is literally "Don't you know that a little yeast affects the whole batch of dough? You must clean out the old yeast so that you can become a new batch of dough. For you are without yeast, because Christ our Passover Lamb has been sacrificed." Leaven is most often used as a metaphor for corrupting influence, especially false teaching.

c 5:8 As translated from the Aramaic. The Greek is "the unleavened bread of sincerity and unhidden reality."

d 5:9 Paul is referring to a previous letter to the Corinthians, known as the lost letter, because a manuscript has never been found.

e 5:9 In the Greek culture of that day, the word *pornos* referred to male prostitution or paramour, although in this context it is not limited to one form of sexual immorality but includes all sexual acts forbidden by Scripture.

isolate yourself from the world entirely![a] [11]But now I'm writing to you so that you would exclude from your fellowship anyone who calls himself a fellow believer and practices sexual immorality, or is consumed with greed, or is an idolater, or is verbally abusive or a drunkard or a swindler. Don't mingle with them or even have a meal with someone like that. [12-13]What right do I have to pronounce judgment on unbelievers? That's God's responsibility. But those who are inside the church family are our responsibility to discern and judge. So it's your duty to remove that wicked one from among you.[b]

Six

Lawsuits between Believers

[1]Furthermore, how dare you take a fellow believer to court! It is wrong to drag him before the unrighteous to settle a legal dispute. Isn't it better to take him before God's holy believers to settle the matter? [2]Don't you realize that we, the holy ones, will judge the universe?[c] If the unbelieving world is under your jurisdiction, you should be fully competent to settle these trivial lawsuits among yourselves. [3]For surely you know that we

---

a 5:10 Or "leave the world." Our Lord Jesus has commanded his disciples to go into all the world and preach the gospel. We do not isolate ourselves from unbelievers but seek opportunities to share the gospel with them.

b 5:13 The Aramaic is "Remove wickedness from among you." See Deuteronomy 17:7. The local church has the authority to discipline erring believers who persist in sin. Under the old covenant, that discipline was physical (execution by stoning), but under the new covenant, church discipline is spiritual. See Matthew 18:15–17.

c 6:2 As translated from the Aramaic.

will one day judge[a] angels, let alone these everyday matters. [4]Don't you realize that you are bringing your issues before civil judges appointed by people who have no standing within the church?[b] [5]What a shame that there is not one within the church[c] who has *the spirit of* wisdom who could arbitrate these disputes and reconcile the offended parties! [6]*It's not right for* a believer to sue a fellow believer—and especially to bring it before the unbelievers.

[7]Don't you realize that when you drag another believer into court you're providing the evidence that you are already defeated? Wouldn't it be better to accept the fact that someone is trying to cheat and take advantage of you, and simply *choose the high road? At times it is better to* just accept injustice and even to let someone take advantage of you, *rather than to expose our conflicts publicly before unbelievers.*[d] [8]But instead you keep cheating and doing wrong to your brothers and sisters, *and then request that unbelievers render their judgment*!

---

a 6:3 The meaning of this is that believers will one day govern over and judge the angelic realm. Our position in Christ is higher than the angels. They are servants; we are sons. Sons rule over servants.

b 6:4 The Greek verb *kathizete* can be interpreted as an ironic imperative instead of a question. This would change the verse to read "Appoint as judges those who have no standing in the church to arbitrate ordinary lawsuits." However, it is more likely a question since *kathizete* is found at the end of the sentence.

c 6:5 This chapter is loaded with irony. Paul here argues that the church must have someone who could discern, sift, weigh, and judge these everyday matters within the body. The irony is that the word for church is *ekklēsia*, which means "governing body," similar to a senate. It was a Greek term used for the gathering of a governing body to promote the welfare of a city. To be a part of an *ekklēsia* (church) implies that there is wisdom and leadership among the group to govern and bring blessing to a city.

d 6:7 Paul does not mean that we should passively acquiesce to abuse from others. Rather, he brings before us a higher principle: It is better to suffer personal injustice than to bring disgrace to Christ by bringing our conflicts before unbelievers. The Spirit of wisdom (Ephesians 1:17) is one of the graces that God pours out upon his people. This anointing of wisdom will empower the body of Christ to bring justice and righteousness into our churches. Most scholars conclude that these disputes were not criminal but issues related to business, personal property, inheritances, default in loan payments to other believers, and the like. See also Matthew 5:25–26 and 18:15–17.

Christian Morality and the Kingdom Realm of God

⁹Surely you must know that people who practice evil cannot possess God's kingdom realm. Stop being deceived!ᵃ People who continue to engage in sexual immorality, idolatry, adultery, sexual perversion,ᵇ homosexuality, ¹⁰fraud, greed, drunkenness, verbal abuse,ᶜ or extortion—these will not inherit God's kingdom realm. ¹¹It's true that some of you once lived in those lifestyles, but now you have been purified from sin,ᵈ made holy, and given a perfect standing before God—all because of the power of the name of the Lord Jesus, the Messiah, and through our union with the Spirit of our God.

¹²It's true that our freedom allows us to do anything, but that doesn't mean that everything we do is good for us. I'm free to do as I choose, but I choose to never be enslaved to anything. ¹³Some have said, "I eat to live and I live to eat!" But God will do away with it all. The body was not created for illicit sex, but to serve and worship our Lord Jesus, who can fill the body with himself.

¹⁴Now the God who raised up our Lord from the grave will awaken and raise us up through his mighty power!

The Body of Christ

¹⁵Don't you know that your bodies belong to Christ as his body parts? Should one presume to take the members of Christ's body and make them into members of a harlot? Absolutely not! ¹⁶Aren't you aware of the fact that when anyone sleeps with a prostitute he becomes a part of her, and she becomes a part of him? For it has been declared:

The two become a single body.ᵉ

---

a 6:9 Or "Make no mistake!"

b 6:9 Or "catamites" or "pederasts" or "child molesters."

c 6:10 Or "slanderers."

d 6:11 Or "washed clean."

e 6:16 See Genesis 2:24. Paul is teaching that sexual intercourse causes an interpersonal union that goes beyond a physical relationship.

[17]But the one who joins[a] himself to the Lord is mingled into one spirit with him. [18]*This is why* you must keep running away from sexual immortality. For every other sin a person commits is external to the body, but immorality involves sinning against your own body.

[19]Have you forgotten that your body is now the sacred temple of the Spirit of Holiness, who lives in you? You don't belong to yourself any longer, for the gift of God, the Holy Spirit, lives inside your sanctuary.[b] [20]You were God's expensive purchase, paid for with tears of blood,[c] so by all means, then, use your body[d] to bring glory to God!

Seven

Sex and Marriage

[1]Now for my response concerning the issues you've asked me to address. *You wrote saying,* "It is proper for a man to live in celibacy."[e] [2]Perhaps. But because of the danger of immorality,[f] each husband should have sexual intimacy with his wife and each wife should have sexual intimacy with her husband. [3]A husband has the responsibility of meeting the sexual needs

---

a 6:17 The Greek verb *kallaō* means "to unite, to knit or weld together, to mingle, or to join together," and "to make two into one."

b 6:19 Or "the in-you Holy Spirit." The Greek word Paul uses for "temple" is actually *naos*, "sanctuary." See Ephesians 2:19–22 and 1 Peter 2:4–5.

c 6:20 As translated from the Aramaic.

d 6:20 The Aramaic and the Textus Receptus adds "and in your spirit."

e 7:1 Or "not to marry." The Aramaic is "It is proper for a husband not to have intimacy with his wife at times." Paul now responds to a series of questions posed by the church of Corinth.

f 7:2 Or "because of immoralities" or "because of prostitutions."

of his wife, and likewise a wife to her husband.[a] [4]Neither the husband nor the wife have exclusive rights to their own bodies, but those rights are to be surrendered to the other. [5]So don't continue to refuse your spouse those rights, except perhaps by mutual agreement for a specified time so that you can both be devoted to prayer.[b] And then you should resume your physical pleasure so that the Adversary cannot take advantage of you because of the desires of your body.[c] [6]I'm not giving you a divine command, but my godly advice.[d] [7]I would wish that all of you could live *unmarried*, just as I do.[e] Yet I understand that we are all decidedly different, with each having a special grace for one thing or another.[f]

[8]So let me say to the unmarried and those who have lost their spouses, it is fine for you to remain single as I am. [9]But if you have no power over your passions, then you should go ahead and marry, for marriage is far better than a continual battle with lust.[g]

Divorce

[10]And to those who are married, I give this charge—which is not mine, but the Lord's[h]—that the wife should not depart from her husband. [11]But

---

a 7:3 The Aramaic (and a few of the oldest Greek manuscripts) reads, "The husband should pay back the love he owes to his wife and the wife to her husband."

b 7:5 Some later manuscripts add "and fasting."

c 7:5 Or "(lack of) self-control." This last sentence is translated from the Aramaic.

d 7:6 Or "concession." There are at least two ways this could be interpreted. 1) Paul is saying that to be married is advisable but not commanded. This seems the most likely because of verse 7. Or 2) Paul is referring to the preceding paragraph, especially regarding the advice of abstinence during seasons of prayer.

e 7:7 The Aramaic is "I wish that all humanity lived in purity as I do." It is possible that Paul was once married and became a widower. Some suggest he had to have been married at the time he persecuted the early church, since only married men could be part of the Sanhedrin and cast a vote. However, there is evidence that some Jewish leaders during his time were committed to celibacy. See Acts 26:10.

f 7:7 Both being single and being married require a special grace from God.

g 7:9 Or "better than to have a fire ever smoldering within them."

h 7:10 Paul is not stating that there is an opposition between what he says, in his teaching as an apostle, and what the Lord says. He is taking our Lord's own teaching from Mark 10:5–12 and bringing it to the people.

if she does, then she should either remain unmarried or reconcile with her husband. And a husband must not divorce his wife. [12]To the rest I say, which is not a saying of the Lord, if a brother has an unbelieving wife and she is content to live with him, he should not divorce her. [13]And if a woman has a husband who is not a believer and he is content to live with her, she should not divorce him. [14]For the unbelieving husband has been made holy by his believing wife. And the unbelieving wife has been made holy by her believing husband *by virtue of his or her sacred union to a believer.*[a] Otherwise, the children from this union would be unclean, but in fact, they are holy.[b] [15]But if the unbelieving spouse wants a divorce, then let it be so. In this situation the believing spouse is not bound[c] *to the marriage,* for God has called us to live in peace.

[16]And wives, for all you know you could one day lead your husband to salvation. Or husbands, how do you know for sure that you could not one day lead your wife to salvation?[d]

Living the Life God Has Assigned

[17]May all believers continue to live the wonderful lives God has called them to live, according to what he assigns for each person, for this is

---

a 7:14 Or "The unbelieving husband is made holy because of the wife, and the unbelieving wife because of her husband." By implication, Paul is making the point that in marriages where one is a believer and one an unbeliever, the spouses should remain together, for the righteous faith of a believer makes the marriage holy. Apparently, because of their desire to serve Christ, some of the Corinthians who had pagan spouses thought it would be best to divorce their spouses and find believing ones. Paul corrects that error and affirms the marriage covenant.

b 7:14 In the concepts of the Old Testament, the entire family is in covenant with God. Therefore, the children of even one believing parent are set apart for God.

c 7:15 Or "enslaved."

d 7:16 Translators are almost equally divided over making this an optimistic possibility versus a pessimistic one. If the pessimistic choice of grammar is chosen, the verse could be translated "Wife, how do you know that you will save your husband? And husband, how do you know that you will save your wife?" Which would infer "It's no use hanging on to a marriage with no hope of converting the unbelieving spouse, for how do you know it would ever happen?" Though both are possible, the translator has chosen the optimistic possibility.

what I teach to believers[a] everywhere. [18]If when you were called *to follow Jesus* you were circumcised, it would be futile to make yourself de-circumcised. And if you were called while yet uncircumcised, there is no need to be circumcised. [19]Your identity *before God* has nothing to do with circumcision or uncircumcision.[b] What really matters is following God's commandments. [20]So everyone should continue to live *faithful* in the situation of life in which they were called *to follow Jesus*.[c] [21]Were you a slave when you heard the call *to follow Jesus*? Don't let that concern you. Even if you can gain your freedom, make the most of the opportunity. [22]For truly, if you are called to a life-union with the Lord, you are already a free man! And those who were called to follow Jesus when they were free are now the Messiah's slaves. [23]Since a great price was paid for your redemption, stop having the mind-set of a slave. [24]Brothers and sisters, we must remain in close communion with God, no matter what our situation was when we were first called to follow Jesus.

Instructions to the Single and Widowed

[25]Now let me address the issue of singleness.[d] I must confess, I have no command to give you that comes directly from the Lord. But let me share my thoughts on the matter, as coming from one who has experienced the mercy[e] of the Lord to keep me faithful to him. [26]Because of the severe

---

a 7:17 Or "in all the churches."

b 7:19 Or "Circumcision is nothing and uncircumcision is nothing." No doubt this statement was a tremendous shock to the Corinthians. To the Jews it would be earthshaking, for circumcision was the outward sign of God's covenant with Abraham and his descendants. Paul, as elsewhere, places the emphasis not on outer things but on an inward transformation that longs to please God.

c 7:20 Paul is teaching that no matter what a person's situation is in life, the real change needed is not just in circumstances, but in a heart that is willing to be faithful to God in all things. We often wish we could be in different circumstances instead of looking for opportunities to serve God where we are.

d 7:25 Or "virgins."

e 7:25 Or "one who has been mercied."

pressure we are in,[a] I recommend you remain as you are. [27]If you are married, stay in the marriage. If you are single,[b] don't rush into marriage. [28]But if you do get married, you haven't sinned.[c] It's just that I would want to spare you the problems you'll face with the extra challenges of being married.

[29]My friends, what I mean is this. The urgency of our times mean that from now on, those who have wives should live as though without them. [30]And those who weep should forget their tears. And those who rejoice will have no time to celebrate. And those who purchase items will have no time to enjoy them. [31]We are to live as those who live in the world system but are not absorbed by it, for the world as we know it is quickly passing away. [32]Because of this, we need to live as free from anxiety as possible.

For a single man is focused on the things of the Lord and how he may please him. [33]But a married man is pulled in two directions, for he is concerned about both the things of God and the things of the world in order to please[d] his wife. [34]And the single woman is focused on the things of the Lord so she can be holy both in body and spirit. But a married woman is concerned about the things of the world and how she may please her husband. [35]I am trying to help you and make things easier for you and not make things difficult, but so that you would have undistracted devotion, serving the Lord constantly with an undivided heart.

[36]However, if a man thinks he is acting inappropriately toward his unmarried daughter who has passed her time and he has not yet given her hand in marriage, it is fitting for him to give her to whomever he

---

a 7:26 Or "impending crisis." Some scholars believe this severe pressure could refer to the great famine of AD 51, while others view it as imminent persecution.

b 7:27 The Aramaic is "If you are divorced, don't seek marriage."

c 7:28 Or "If you (men) do get married it is not sin, and if a (female) virgin marries, she hasn't sinned." The translation combines both statements with *brothers and sisters.*

d 7:33 The Aramaic is "beautify."

chooses; he does not sin and she may get married.[a] [37]On the other hand, if a man stands firm in his heart to remain single, and is under no compulsion to get married but has control over his passions and is determined to remain celibate, he has chosen well. [38]So then, the one who marries his fiancée does well and the one who chooses not to marry her does better.

Remarriage

[39]A wife is bound *by the marriage covenant* as long as her husband is living. But if the husband dies, she is free to marry again as she desires—but, of course, he should be a believer in the Lord. [40]However, in my opinion (and I think that I too have the Spirit of God), she would be happier if she remained single.

Love Is Greater than Knowledge

[1]Now let me address the issue of food offered in sacrifice to idols. It seems that everyone believes his own opinion is right on this matter.[b]

---

a 7:36 As translated from the Aramaic and implied in the Greek. This is arguably one of the most difficult verses to translate in all the New Testament. You will find many possible translations and interpretations of this passage. The Greek text can be translated "If a man has decided to serve God as a single person, yet changes his mind and finds himself in love with a woman, although he never intended to marry, let him go ahead and marry her; it is not a sin to do so." Or "If a man thinks he is acting inappropriately toward his fiancée (or virgin), if she is past the high point (or bloom of youth) or if his passions are too strong, and if it appears to him as necessary, then let him do as he desires; it is not sin." There are many possible translations of this difficult Greek text, which is loaded with cultural implications for the first-century church. Consulting a variety of translations is recommended.

b 8:1 Or "we all have knowledge."

How easily we get puffed up over our opinions! But love builds up the structure *of our new life*.[a] [2]If anyone thinks of himself as a know-it-all, he still has a lot to learn. [3]But if a person passionately loves God, he will possess the knowledge of God.[b]

[4]Concerning food sacrificed as offerings to idols, we all know that an idol is nothing, for there is no God but one.[c] [5]Although there may be many so-called gods in this world, and in heaven there may be many "gods," "lords," and "masters," [6]yet for us there is only one God—the Father. He is the source of all things, and our lives are lived for him. And there is one Lord, Jesus, the Anointed One, through whom we and all things exist.

[7]But not everyone has this revelation. For some were formerly idolaters, who consider idols as real and living. That's why they consider the food offered to that "god" as defiled. And their weak consciences become defiled if they eat it. [8]Yes, we know that what you eat will not bring you closer to God. You are no better if you don't eat certain foods and no better if you do. [9]But you must be careful that the liberty you exercise in eating food offered to idols doesn't offend the weak believers. [10]For if a believer with a weak conscience sees you, who have a greater understanding, dining in an idol's temple, won't this be a temptation to him to violate his own conscience[d] and eat food offered to idols? [11]So, in effect, by exercising your understanding of freedom, you have ruined

---

a 8:1 That is, knowledge may make a person look important, but it is only through love that we reach our full maturity. It is simply "Love builds up. It builds up our lives, our churches, our families, and others. Love is the most powerful substance for building what will last forever.

b 8:3 Explicit in the Aramaic and implied in the Greek, which can also be translated, "is known (acknowledged) by God."

c 8:4 See Deuteronomy 6:4.

d 8:10 Or "have his conscience built up." Ironically, this is the same Greek word Paul used in verse 1 for love *builds up*. The implication is that the weak believer will be emboldened to violate his conscience by watching a more mature believer freely eating food offered to idols.

this weak believer,[a] a brother for whom Christ has died! [12]And when you offend weaker believers by wounding their consciences in this way, you also offend[b] the Anointed One!

[13]So I conclude that if my eating certain food deeply offends[c] my brother and hinders his advance in Christ, I will never eat it again. I don't want to be guilty of causing my brother or sister to be wounded and defeated.

Nine

Paul's Apostolic Freedom

[1] Am I not completely free and unrestrained? *Absolutely!* Am I not an apostle? *Of course!* Haven't I had a personal encounter with our Jesus face-to-face—*and continue to see him?*[d] *Emphatically yes!* Aren't you all the proof of my ministry in the Lord?[e] *Certainly!* [2]If others do not

---

a 8:11 This is because the "freedom" of the mature could lead the immature believer back into what he feels is idol worship.

b 8:12 That is, "They bring an offense against the teachings of Christ," as translated from the Aramaic. The Greek is "When you sin against a weaker believer...you also sin against Christ."

c 8:13 The Greek word *skandalizō* (from which we get our English word *scandal*) means "to throw a snare in front of someone purposely to trip them up."

d 9:1 As implied by the perfect active indicative. Paul has *seen the Lord,* but the effects of that "seeing" continue on in full force (i.e., "I continue to have him in my sight").

e 9:1 These four forceful rhetorical questions are emphatic in the Greek construction, which means they each demand an answer in the affirmative. Although some commentators view these four questions as qualifications of an apostle, there is no indication that this is indeed the purpose of his questions. Paul is defending his apostleship, not listing qualifications of apostles. The seven arguments he makes in defense of his apostleship recognize me as their apostle, as least you are bound to do so, for now your lives are joined to the Lord. You are the *living proof*, the certificate of my apostleship.

³So to those who want to continually criticize my apostolic ministry, here's my statement of defense.[a] ⁴Don't we apostles have the right to be supported financially?[b] ⁵Don't we have the right to travel accompanied by our believing wives *and be supported as a couple*, as do the other apostles, such as Peter the Rock and the Lord's brothers?[c] ⁶*Of course we do!*[d] Or is it only Barnabas and I who have no right to stop working for a living?[e]

Responsibility to Financially Support God's Servants

⁷Who serves in the military at his own expense? Who plants a vineyard and does not enjoy the grapes for himself? Who would nurture and shepherd a flock and never get to drink its fresh milk? ⁸Am I merely giving you my own opinions, or does the Torah teach the same things? ⁹For it is written in the law of Moses:

> **You should never put a muzzle over the mouth of an ox**
> **while he is treading out the grain.**[f]

---

are: 1) He enjoys freedom from all bondage, both from the world and religion (verse 1), 2) He had face-to-face encounters with Jesus (verse 1 and 15:8), 3) The formation of the church of Corinth validates his apostleship (verses 1–2 and Acts 18), 4) His unselfish lifestyle resulted in not demanding to be paid for his ministry (verses 3–15), 5) He was given a divine stewardship (verses 16–18), 6) He was determined to win everyone through the gospel of Christ (verses 19–23), and 7) He lived a disciplined life in order to succeed in the obstacle course of ministry for Christ (verses 24–27).

a 9:3 The Aramaic is quite blunt: "Those who judge me I rebuke in (the) spirit."

b 9:3 Or "to eat and drink," a euphemism to describe financial support.

c 9:5 See Mark 6:3 and John 2:12.

d 9:6 Made explicit from the Greek disjunctive particle.

e 9:6 Apostles were usually cared for and financially supported by the church so they didn't have to engage in secular work for their wages, although Paul and Barnabas, on different occasions, supported themselves without being a burden to the congregations (see verses 12–15).

f 9:9 See Deuteronomy 25:4 and 1 Timothy 5:18.

Tell me, is God only talking about oxen here? [10]Doesn't he also give us this principle so that we won't withhold support from his workers?[a] It was written so that we would understand that the one *spiritually* "plowing" and *spiritually* "treading out the grain" also labors with the expectation of enjoying the harvest. [11]So, if we've sowed many spiritual gifts[b] among you, is it too much to expect to reap material gifts from you? [12]And if you have supported others, don't we rightfully deserve this privilege even more?

But as you know, we haven't used that right. Instead, we have continued to support ourselves[c] so that we would never be a hindrance to the spread of the gospel of Christ. [13]Don't you know that the priests[d] employed in sacred duty in the temple[e] are provided for by temple resources? And the priests who serve at the altar receive a portion of the offerings?[f] [14]In the same way, the Lord has directed those who proclaim the gospel to receive their living by the gospel. As for me, I've preferred to never use any of these rights for myself. [15]And keep in mind that I'm not writing all this because I'm hinting that you should support me.

Paul Renounces His Rights for the Sake of the Gospel

Actually, I'd rather die than to have anyone rob me of this joyous reason for boasting![g] [16]For you see, even though I proclaim the good news, I can't take the credit for my labors, for I am compelled to fulfill my duty by completing this work. It would be agony to me if I did not constantly preach

---

a 9:10 Or "Doesn't he say this for our sake (as apostles)?"

b 9:11 The Greek word *pneumatikos* is often used for spiritual gifts, not just spiritual blessings. See 1 Corinthians 12:1 and 14:1. The Aramaic is explicit: "Since we have planted the Spirit in you, we should harvest financially from you."

c 9:12 Or "We have endured all things."

d 9:13 Or "those who work with sacred things."

e 9:13 The Aramaic word for *temple* is "house of blessing."

f 9:13 Or "what is offered on the altar." See Leviticus 6:9–11, 19.

g 9:15 Paul uses the rhetorical device of abruptly breaking off his statement ("I would rather die than—"). This is known as an aposiopesis, meant to intensify the importance of having the joy of boasting in the fact that Paul provided for his own needs in ministry.

the gospel! [17]If it were my own idea to preach as a way to make a living, I would expect to be paid. Since it's not my idea but God's, who commissioned me, I am entrusted with the stewardship of the gospel *whether or not I'm paid.* [18]So then, where is my reward? It is found in continually depositing the good news *into people's hearts*, without obligation, free of charge, and not insisting on my rights to be financially supported.

Paul, a Servant to All

[19]Now, even though I am free from obligations to others,[a] I *joyfully* make myself a servant to all in order to win as many converts as possible. [20]I became Jewish to the Jewish people in order to win them *to the Messiah.* I became like one under the law to gain the people who were stuck under the law, even though I myself am not under the law. [21]And to those who are without the Jewish laws, I became like them, as one without the Jewish laws, in order to win them, although I'm not outside the law of God but under the law of Christ. [22]I became "weak" to the weak to win the weak. I have adapted to the culture of every place I've gone[b] so that I could more easily win people to Christ. [23]I've done all this so that I would become God's partner for the sake of the gospel.[c]

Paul's Disciplined Lifestyle

[24]Isn't it obvious that all runners on the racetrack[d] keep on running to win, but only one receives the victor's prize? Yet each one of you must

---

a 9:19 That is, Paul lived free from the obligation of pleasing those who paid him a salary. He lived by faith, yet he still became the servant of all.

b 9:22 Or "I have become all things to all different kinds of people"; that is, he adapted culturally wherever he ministered.

c 9:23 Paul is declaring the five motivating principles for his ministry: 1) Always start by finding common ground with those you want to reach. 2) Avoid projecting to others that you are a know-it-all. 3) Accept everyone regardless of his or her issues. 4) Be sensitive to the culture of others. 5) Use every opportunity to share the good news of Jesus Christ with people.

d 9:24 Or "the runners in a stadium." This refers to the Pan-Hellenic stadium near Corinth where the Isthmian games were held.

run the race to be victorious. [25]A true athlete will be disciplined in every respect, practicing constant self-control in order to win a laurel wreath that quickly withers. But we run our race to win a victor's crown that will last forever. [26]For that reason, I don't run just for exercise[a] or box like one throwing aimless punches, [27]but I train like a champion athlete. I subdue my body[b] and get it under my control, so that after preaching the good news to others I myself won't be disqualified.

Ten

Learning from Israel's Failures

[1]My dear fellow believers, you need to understand that all of our Jewish ancestors *who walked through a wilderness long ago* were under the glory cloud[c] and passed through the waters of the sea on both sides. [2]They were all baptized[d] into the cloud of glory, into the fellowship of Moses, and into the sea. [3]They all ate the same heavenly manna[e] [4]and

---

a 9:26 Or "I don't run aimlessly." That is, Paul ran with his eyes on the goal of ending well.

b 9:27 Or "I beat my body black and blue." This is an obvious metaphor of placing the desires of one's body as second place to the desires of the Holy Spirit. See Romans 8:13.

c 10:1 The cloud of glory is a picture of the Holy Spirit.

d 10:2 Or "baptized themselves." There are at least eight distinct baptisms mentioned in the New Testament: 1) the baptism of John (John 1:31–33), 2) Christ's baptism (John 3:22), 3) a baptism of suffering (Luke 12:50), 4) a baptism into the cloud of glory (1 Corinthians 10:2), 5) a baptism into the sea (a picture of redemption—1 Corinthians 10:2), 6) believer's baptism in water (Matthew 28:19; Acts 2:38–41), 7) baptism into Christ and into his body (1 Corinthians 12:13; Galatians 3:27), and 8) baptism in the Holy Spirit (Matthew 3:11–14; Acts 1:5; 11:16; 19:2–3). See also Hebrews 6:2.

e 10:3 Or "spiritual food." See Exodus 16, Psalm 78:24–25, and John 6:31–48.

drank water from the same spiritual rock[a] that traveled with them—and that Rock[b] was Christ himself. [5]Yet God was not pleased with most of them, and their dead bodies were scattered around the wilderness.[c]

[6]Now, all these things serve as types and pictures for us—lessons that teach us not to fail in the same way by callously craving worthless things [7]and practicing idolatry, as some of them did. For it is written:

The people settled in to their unrestrained revelry, with feasting and drinking, then they rose up and became wildly out of control![d]

[8]Neither should we commit sexual immorality, as some of them did, which caused the death of twenty-three thousand[e] on a single day. [9]Nor should we ever provoke the Lord,[f] as some of them did by putting him to outrageous tests that resulted in their death from snakebites day after day.[g] [10]And we must not embrace their ways by complaining—grumbling with discontent, as many of them did,[h] and were killed by the destroyer![i]

[11]All the tests they endured on their way through the wilderness are a symbolic picture, an example that provides us with a warning so that

---

a 10:4 See Exodus 17:6, Numbers 20:7–21, and Psalm 78:15.

b 10:4 Christ is the Anointed Rock of truth and the Rock of shelter. The people drank of his living water. The miracle of the Rock of Christ provided them with water wherever they journeyed. He is a fountain that never runs dry, for he will never leave us alone in a wilderness.

c 10:5 The Aramaic is "They failed (the test) in the wilderness."

d 10:7 Although most translations have "They rose up to play," this is misleading. To translate the Greek word *paizō* in this context is extremely difficult. However, because of the next verse, it appears Paul is saying that they rose up after feasting and drinking to fall into immorality. Although *paizō* could be translated "They rose up to sport" or "They rose up to hilarity," it seems that sexual immorality is the more likely inference here. The Aramaic word can be translated "carouse."

e 10:8 Some manuscripts have "twenty-four thousand." See Numbers 25:9.

f 10:9 Some manuscripts have "Christ."

g 10:9 See Numbers 21:5–9.

h 10:10 In the Pentateuch there are at least sixteen occasions of the people of Israel murmuring. Believers today have even more spiritual blessings than Israel experienced in the wilderness, which would make our complaining even more odious.

i 10:10 Or "the destroying angel."

we can learn through what they experienced. For we live in a time when the purpose of all the ages past is now completing its goal within us.[a] ¹²So beware if you think it could never happen to you, lest your pride becomes your downfall.

The Way of Escape

¹³We all experience[b] times of testing,[c] which is normal for every human being. But God will be faithful to you. He will screen and filter the severity, nature, and timing of every test or trial you face[d] so that you can bear it. And each test is an opportunity to trust him more, for along with every trial God has provided for you a way of escape[e] that will bring you out of it victoriously.[f]

Communion

¹⁴My cherished friends, keep on running far away from idolatry. ¹⁵I know I am writing to thoughtful people, so carefully consider what I say. ¹⁶For when we pray for the blessing of the communion cup, isn't this our co-participation with the blood of Jesus?[g] And the bread that we distribute, isn't this the bread of our co-participation with the body of Christ?[h]

---

a 10:11 As translated from the Aramaic. The Greek is "The end of the ages has arrived upon us."

b 10:13 Or "which has fastened onto you."

c 10:13 Or "temptation."

d 10:13 That is, God's faithfulness and grace will limit the severity of every test and prevent you from being tested beyond your ability to cope. Unlimited grace is available for every believer who faces hardship, temptations, and seasons of difficulty.

e 10:13 Or "an exodus." Trust in God's faithfulness is the way of escape that empowers us to overcome every difficulty we may experience. We are not told that every difficulty will be removed from our lives, but that God's grace provides an exit path.

f 10:13 Or "God bears up under you to take you out of danger (Greek hupophero)" or "God provides a way of escape so that you may be empowered to endure it." God's faithfulness gives us both a way of escape and the power to endure.

g 10:16 The Aramaic is "the presence of the blood of Jesus."

h 10:16 The Aramaic is "the presence of the body of the Messiah."

[17]For although we're many, we become one loaf of bread and one body as we feast together[a] on one loaf.

[18]Consider the people of Israel *when they fell into idolatry*. When they ate the sacrifices offered to the gods, weren't they becoming communal participants in what was sacrificed? [19]Now, am I saying that idols and the sacrifices offered to them have any value? [20]Absolutely not! However, I am implying that when an unbeliever offers a sacrifice to an idol, it is not offered to the true God but to a demon. I don't want you to be participants with demons! [21]You can't drink from the cup of the Lord and the cup of demons. You can't feast at the table of the Lord and feast[b] at the table of demons. [22]Who would ever want to arouse the Lord's jealousy? Is that something you think you're strong enough to endure?[c]

Living for God's Glory

[23]*You say,* "*Under grace* there are no rules and we're free to do anything we please." Not exactly. Because not everything promotes growth in others. Your slogan "We're allowed to do anything we choose" may be true—but not everything causes the spiritual advancement of others. [24]So don't always seek what is best for you at the expense of another. [25]Yes, you are free to eat anything without worrying about your conscience, [26]for the earth and all its abundance belongs to the Lord.[d]

[27]So if an unbeliever invites you to dinner, go ahead and eat whatever is served, without asking questions concerning where it came from.[e] [28]But if he goes out of his way to inform you that the meat was actually an offering sacrificed to idols, then you should pass, not only for his sake but because of his conscience. [29]I'm talking about someone else's

---

a 10:17 The Aramaic is "We are nourished by that one loaf of bread."

b 10:21 Or "participate," which is the Greek word *metaecho,* or "echo with."

c 10:22 Or "Are we really stronger than he is?"

d 10:25 See Psalm 24:1, 50:12, and 89:11.

e 10:26 Or "questions of conscience."

conscience, not yours. What good is there in doing what you please if it's condemned by someone else?

[30]So if I voluntarily participate, why should I be judged for celebrating my freedom?[a] [31]Whether you eat or drink, live your life in a way that glorifies and honors God. [32]And make sure you're not offending Jews or Greeks or any part of God's assembly *over your personal preferences.* [33]*Follow my example,* for I try to please everyone in all things, rather than putting my liberty first. I sincerely attempt to do anything I can so that others may be saved.

Eleven

Head Coverings

[1]I want you to pattern your lives after me, just as I pattern mine after Christ. [2]And I give you full credit for always keeping me in mind as you follow carefully the substance of my instructions[b] that I've taught you. [3]But I want you to understand that Christ is the source[c] of every human

---

a 10:30 Or "eating food that I gave thanks for."

b 11:2 Or "traditions" or "guidelines." It is likely that the instructions Paul refers to here are regarding their public worship. This would include cultural customs about church order and not necessarily doctrinal matters.

c 11:3 Or "head." Although the Greek word *kephale,* found three times in this verse, can be "head," it is used figuratively. It is not used in Greek literature or Scripture as "head over," "chief," or "ruler." To say that Christ is the head of every man means that he is the source of our life and faith as the head of the body of Christ. Christ is the "head" as in the head of a river. See also verse 8–9, which support this. The source of the woman is man, for Eve was taken from Adam. The source of the Messiah is God, for he provided a virgin birth for Christ and formed his body and fulfilled the prophecies God spoke about him.

alive, and Adam was the source of Eve,[a] and God is the source of the Messiah.

[4]Any man *who leads public worship,*[b] and prays or prophesies with a shawl hanging down over his head, shows disrespect to his head, *which is Christ.* [5]And if any woman *in a place of leadership* within the church prays or prophesies *in public* with her long hair disheveled,[c] she shows disrespect to her head, *which is her husband,* for this would be the same as having her head shaved. [6]If a woman who wants to be in leadership will not conform to the customs of what is proper for women,[d] she might as well cut off her hair. But if it's disgraceful for her to have her hair cut off[e] or her head shaved, let her cover her head.

[7]A man *in leadership* is under no obligation to have his head covered *in the public gatherings,* because he is the portrait of God and reflects his glory. The woman, on the other hand, reflects the glory of her husband, [8]for man was not created from woman but woman from man.[f] [9]By the same token, the man was not created because the woman needed him;

Another possible translation of verse 3 is "Christ has responsibility over all men, as the husband has responsibility for his wife, and God the Father has responsibility over Christ."

a 11:3 As translated from the Aramaic.

b 11:4 Implied in both the Aramaic and the Greek, as also in verse 5. This section (verses 3–16) is not focused on marriage or the role of women in the church, but on proper attitudes of reverence and conduct in public worship. Paul's discussion here would have made obvious sense within the cultural standards of the Corinthians. It is a continuation of Paul's teaching that if our conduct offends and divides the church, we are to change our ways in order to promote unity among the believers. See chapter 10 verses 27–33.

c 11:5 Or "unbound," as translated from the Aramaic. The Greek is "with her head uncovered." The Greek word *akatakalyptos* is commonly translated as "unveiled" or "uncovered." However, the Greek LXX of Leviticus 13:45 uses the word *akatakalyptos* in saying that a person who has "leprosy" signals to the world his disease by staying dirty and keeping his hair "disheveled." Notice also that Paul affirms the right of women to pray and prophesy in public worship services.

d 11:6 Or "So, if a women will not wear a head covering, ..."

e 11:6 That is, "having her hair cut off (like a prostitute)," which was the common practice in Corinth. For the public worship of that era, a woman would have her long hair braided and covered up so she would not be mistaken as a cult priestess of Isis or Dionysus.

f 11:8 See Genesis 2:21–23 and 1 Timothy 2:13.

the woman was created because the man needed her.[a] [10]For this reason she should have authority over the head because of the angels.[b]

[11]So then, I have to insist that in the Lord, neither is woman inferior to man nor is man inferior to woman.[c] [12]For just as woman was taken from the side of man, in the same way man is taken from the *womb of* woman. God, as the source of all things, *designed it this way.*

[13]So then you can decide for yourselves—is it proper for a woman to pray to God with her hair unbound?[d] [14]Doesn't our long-established cultural tradition teach us that if a man has long hair that is *ornamentally arranged* it invites disgrace, but if a woman has long hair that is *ornamentally arranged* it is her glory? [15]This is because long hair is the endowment that God has given her as a head covering.[e]

[16]If someone wants to quarrel about this, I want you to know that we have no intention[f] to start an argument, neither I nor the congregations of God.

---

a 11:9 See Genesis 2:18. In Christ, there is no fundamental difference between man and woman, as both were created by God with different roles and personalities. Although the first woman, Eve, came from Adam, every other man came from a woman (mother). To use Genesis 2:18 to say that women are inferior to men is equal to saying that all men are inferior to their mothers.

b 11:10 This literal translation is one of the most difficult verses in all the New Testament to translate and to interpret properly. Scholars and translators are divided in how to express this verse with proper meaning. First, Paul uses the Greek word *exousia* (authority), which is used for the authority of God, kings, and rulers, and can be translated "might" or "right." It never occurs as a metaphor speaking of a piece of apparel. This is not a symbol of authority, but true authority on *the* (not her) head under which she ministers. Before Pentecost, the woman was not seen as anyone with authority, but at Pentecost the Holy Spirit fell upon men and women, giving each person the authority to take the gospel with power to the ends of the earth and prophesy under the direction of the Holy Spirit. The gospels both begin and end with a visitation of angels to women. The angel Gabriel came to Mary and the angels of God greeted the women at the empty tomb. However, the Aramaic word used here is a homonym that can mean both "power" and "covering/veil." This may explain the variation of the Greek texts.

c 11:11 As translated from the Aramaic and implied in the Greek.

d 11:13 As translated from the Aramaic. The Greek is "with her head uncovered."

e 11:15 Or "prayer shawl." The Greek word *peribolaion* is translated in the Deuteronomy 22:12 LXX as "prayer shawl."

f 11:16 Or "custom."

The Lord's Table

¹⁷Now, on this next matter, I wish I could commend you, but I cannot, because when you meet together as a church family, it is doing more harm than good! ¹⁸I've been told many times that when you meet as a congregation, divisions and cliques emerge—and to some extent, this doesn't surprise me. ¹⁹Differences of opinion are unavoidable, yet they will reveal which ones among you truly have God's approval.ᵃ

²⁰When all of *your house churches*ᵇ gather as one church family, you are not really properly celebrating the Lord's Supper.ᶜ ²¹For when it comes time to eat, some gobble down their food before anything is given to others—one is left hungry while others become drunk!ᵈ ²²Don't you all have homes where you can eat and drink? Don't you realize that you're showing a superior attitude by humiliating those who have nothing? Are you trying to show contempt for God's beloved church? How should I address this appropriately? If you're looking for my approval, you won't find it!

²³I have handed down to you what came to me by direct revelation from the Lord himself. The same night in which he was handed over,ᵉ he took bread ²⁴and gave thanks. Then he distributed it to the disciples and said, "Take it and eat your fill.ᶠ It is my body, which is given for you.

---

a 11:19 Differences of opinion between believers expose our hearts. Mature ones will overlook offenses and faults in order to maintain the precious unity of the body of Christ. Immature ones will cause splits, divisions, and cliques around their respective opinions. The ones whom God approves are those whose hearts remain pure in spite of petty differences.

b 11:20 Implied both in the text and by the cultural context of the day.

c 11:20 Paul is implying that it is the Lord's Supper, not merely a meal for favored ones. Jesus is hosting the meal for the benefit of all every time we gather for communion.

d 11:21 Apparently, the church of Corinth was divided between the "haves" and the "have nots." Those who were wealthy would feast and become drunk, while those who had very little went hungry. The precious unity of the church was spoiled by this behavior. These shared meals were called "love feasts" (Jude 12).

e 11:23 Or "betrayed." Paul is using a play on words in the Greek text. He *handed down* to us the instructions for the Lord's Table, but the Lord was *handed over* to his accusers.

f 11:24 As translated from the Aramaic, which means "Eat and be satisfied."

Do this to remember me." [25]He did the same with the cup *of wine* after supper and said, "This cup seals the new covenant with my blood. Drink it—and whenever you drink this, do it to remember me."

[26]Whenever you eat this bread and drink this cup, you are retelling the story, proclaiming our Lord's death until he comes. [27]For this reason, whoever eats the bread or drinks the cup of the Lord in the wrong spirit will be guilty of dishonoring the body and blood of the Lord. [28]So let each individual first evaluate his own attitude and only then eat the bread and drink the cup. [29]For continually eating and drinking with a wrong spirit[a] will bring judgment upon yourself by not recognizing the body.[b] [30]This insensitivity is why many of you are weak, chronically ill, and some even dying.[c] [31]If you do not sit in judgment of others, you will avoid judgment yourself.[d] [32]But when we are judged, it is the Lord's training, so that we will not be condemned along with the world.

[33]So then, my fellow believers, when you assemble as one to share a meal, show respect for one another and wait for all to be served.[e] [34]If you are that hungry, eat at home first, so that when you gather together you will not bring judgment upon yourself.

When I come to you, I will answer the other questions you asked me *in your letter.*

---

a 11:29 Or "unworthily" or "irreverently."

b 11:29 Some manuscripts have "the Lord's body." This can be understood in at least two ways. It may refer to not recognizing the bread as Christ's body given in sacrifice, or not recognizing Christ's body on earth, the church. To properly discern the Lord's body, which was beaten and bruised for our healing, would mean we would not be weak or sick or die prematurely.

c 11:30 Or "asleep," a metaphor for death.

d 11:31 As translated from the Aramaic. The Greek is "If we have examined ourselves, we should not be judged."

e 11:33 The Aramaic is "strengthen (encourage) one another."

Twelve

Spiritual Gifts

¹My fellow believers, I don't want you to be confused about spiritual real-ities.ᵃ ²For you know full well that when you were unbelievers you were often led astrayᵇ in one way or another by your worship of idols, which are incapable of talking with you. ³Therefore, I want to impart to you an understanding of the following:

No one speaking by the Spirit of Godᶜ would ever say, "Jesus is the accursed one."

No one can say, "Jesus is the Lord Yahweh,"ᵈ unless the Holy Spirit is speaking through him.ᵉ

⁴It is the same Holy Spirit who continues to distribute many different varieties of gifts.ᶠ

⁵The Lord Yahweh is one,ᵍ and he is the one who apportions to believers different varieties of ministries.ʰ

---

a 12:1 The Greek word *pneumatikos* is "*spiritual* (things)," with the implication of spiritual realities or spiritual gifts. Some scholars believe that "spirituals" may refer to spiritual persons.

b 12:2 Or "carried (snatched) away."

c 12:3 Some scholars believe this "speaking in the Spirit of God" refers to speaking in tongues.

d 12:3 As translated from the Aramaic. The Greek language has no equivalent for "Lord Yahweh" and uses the word *kurios*, which means "sir, master, wealthy landowner, boss" and is sometimes used for demons. The Aramaic is preferred. It is by divine revelation that one begins to see that the Lord Yahweh is none other than our Lord Jesus Christ.

e 12:3 Or "except by union with the Holy Spirit."

f 12:4 The nine gifts distributed by the Holy Spirit listed here include: the word of wisdom, the word of knowledge, the gift of faith, gifts of healing, miraculous powers, prophecy, discerning of spirits, speaking in different kinds of tongues, and interpretation of tongues. See verses 7–11.

g 12:5 As translated from the Aramaic. See also Deuteronomy 6:4.

h 12:5 See Ephesians 4:7–16. The ministries Jesus apportions by grace are apostles, proph-

⁶The same God distributes different kinds of miracles[a] that accomplish different results through each believer's gift and ministry as he energizes and activates them.

⁷Each believer is given continuous revelation[b] by the Holy Spirit to benefit not just himself but all.[c]

Varieties of Spiritual Gifts

⁸For example:

The Spirit gives to one the gift of the word of wisdom.[d]

To another, the same Spirit gives the gift of the word of revelation knowledge.[e]

---

ets, evangelists, pastors, and teachers.

a 12:6 As translated from the Aramaic, which can also be translated "powers."

b 12:7 As translated from the Aramaic and implied in the Greek word *phanerosis* ("the clear display in light," or "public manifestations").

c 12:7 To summarize, God the Father, the Son, and the Spirit delights to give spiritual gifts to his people, the bride of Christ. These gifts are imparted by God to every believer upon conversion as the Holy Spirit chooses (verse 11). They will confirm the Word of God and expand the kingdom of God. Spiritual gifts can be neglected and misused, but they remain the divine power source for Christ's body on the earth. Through teaching, evangelizing, prophesying, and demonstrating the miraculous, God uses his people to expand his kingdom and to establish righteousness on the earth through the proper use of the gifts he has given. There is no place in Scripture or church history where these gifts were taken away or removed from the body of Christ. The church moves forward through these divine gifts. Spiritual gifts do not replace the Word of God, but the Word of God will spread and flourish as the fully equipped body of Christ operates in the wise use of God's enabling power.

d 12:8 Or "the message (Greek *logos*) of wisdom." This is a revelation gift of the Holy Spirit to impart an understanding of strategy and insight that only God can give. This is more than simply wisdom, but the clearly crafted *word of wisdom* to unlock the hearts of people and free the corporate body to move forward under God's direction. This gift will express the wisdom of the Holy Spirit, not of man. The best examples of this gift were 1) when Jesus saw Nathaniel under the fig tree and knew his true character as a man without guile and 2) when Jesus spoke to the woman at the well and unlocked her heart with the words "Go bring your husband." See John 1 and John 4.

e 12:8 The gift of the message (Greek *logos*) of revelation knowledge has been defined by some as the Holy Spirit's impartation through an impression, a vision, or his voice that gives understanding of a person or situation that cannot be known through the natural

[9]And to another, the same Spirit gives the gift of faith.[a]

And to another, the same Spirit gives gifts of healing.[b]

[10]And to another the power to work miracles.[c]

And to another the gift of prophecy.[d]

And to another the gift to discern what the Spirit is speaking.[e]

And to another the gift of speaking different kinds of tongues.

And to another the gift of interpretation of tongues.

[11]Remember, it is the same Holy Spirit who distributes, activates, and operates these different gifts as he chooses for each believer.[f]

One Body with Many Parts

[12]Just as the human body is one, though it has many parts that together form one body, so too is Christ.[g] [13]For by one Spirit we all were immersed

---

mind of man. It may be exercised in the prayer for healing. This revelation knowledge is seen in Saul's healing of blindness in Acts 9 and in Acts 10–11 with Peter's revelation knowledge of Cornelius's servants outside his door and the subsequent salvation of Cornelius and his household. The word of revelation knowledge could also include knowing facts that are unknown to the speaker, such as names, dates, or events to come.

a 12:9 This is the supernatural power of faith released in a believer to do the miracle works of God on the earth.

b 12:9 This is the supernatural power of God released through a believer to heal the sick.

c 12:10 This includes the divine ability to still a storm, feed a multitude, walk on water, cast out demons, turn water into wine, and raise the dead. This gift was one of the distinctive marks of an apostle. See 2 Corinthians 12:12.

d 12:10 This gift is a supernatural ability, given by the Holy Spirit, to speak the word of God in proclamation and at times in predicting the future. This is one gift that every believer should desire and never despise. See 1 Corinthians 14:1; 1 Thessalonians 5:19–20; 1 Timothy 1:18 and 4:14.

e 12:10 This gift imparts divine discernment to know if a prophetic message is from the Holy Spirit or from a human or demonic source. See Acts 5:3. Discernment is greatly needed in the church today to hear the voice of the Lord clearly and to know when defilement is attempting to enter the assembly.

f 12:11 Spiritual gifts are given by the Holy Spirit at any time to anyone he chooses.

g 12:12 Christ is now a body with many parts. The human body of Jesus is glorified and enthroned in heaven. So also is the body of Christ. We are co-enthroned with him (Romans 8:29–30; Ephesians 2:6; Colossians 3:1–4), but we continue to exist on earth to represent him to the world.

and mingled into one single body.[a] And no matter our status—whether we are Jews or non-Jews, oppressed or free—we are all privileged to drink deeply of the same Holy Spirit.[b]

[14]In fact, the human body is not one single part but rather many parts *mingled into one.* [15]So if the foot were to say, "Since I'm not a hand, I'm not a part of the body," it's forgetting that it is still a vital part of the body. [16]And if the ear were to say, "Since I'm not an eye, I'm not really a part of the body," it's forgetting that it is still an important part of the body.

[17]*Think of it this way.* If the whole body were just an eyeball, how could it hear sounds? And if the whole body were just an ear, how could it smell different fragrances? [18]But God has carefully designed each member and placed it in the body to function as he desires.[c] [19]*A diversity is required,* for if the body consisted of one single part, there wouldn't be a body at all! [20]So now we see that there are many differing parts and functions, but one body.

No Competition for Importance within the Body

[21]It would be wrong for the eye to say to the hand, "I don't need you," and equally wrong if the head said to the foot, "I don't need you." [22]In fact, the weaker our parts, the more vital and essential they are.[d] [23]The body parts we think are less honorable we treat with greater respect.

---

a 12:13 This is not a baptism into the Spirit (Matthew 3:6) but a baptism into the body of Christ. Upon conversion, the Holy Spirit does four things for every believer: 1) He gives us new birth (regeneration—see John 3:5 and Titus 3:5). 2) He comes to live inside us (indwelling—see Romans 8:9). 3) He places us into the body as a member of Christ's body on the earth (spiritual baptism—see 1 Corinthians 12:13). 4) He seals us as the possession of Christ until the redemption of our human body (see Ephesians 1:13–14; 4:30).

b 12:13 To "drink deeply" of the Spirit is the same as receiving his power and gifts until rivers of living water flow from the inside of us. See John 3:34; 7:37.

c 12:18 Every believer should be content with the place within the body God has placed him. And God is pleased when we serve him with joy in every activity or ministry that we engage in for the sake of the body.

d 12:22 Paul is, no doubt, speaking of our internal organs: liver, heart, lungs, etc.

And the body parts that need to be covered in public we treat with propriety and clothe them. ²⁴But some of our body parts don't require as much attention. Instead, God has mingled the body parts together, giving greater honor to the "lesser" members who lacked it. ²⁵*He has done this intentionally* so that every member would look after the others with mutual concern, and so that there will be no division in the body. ²⁶In that way, whatever happens to one member happens to all. If one suffers, everyone suffers. If one is honored, everyone rejoices.

One Body with Different Gifts

²⁷You are the body of the Anointed One, and each of you is a unique and vital part of it. ²⁸God has placed in the church the following:

First apostles,
second prophets,
third teachers,
then those with gifts of miracles, gifts of divine healing,
gifts of revelation knowledge,ᵃ gifts of leadership,ᵇ
and gifts of different kinds of tongues.

²⁹Not everyone is an apostle or a prophet or a teacher. Not everyone performs miracles ³⁰or has gifts of healing or speaks in tongues or interprets tongues. ³¹But you should all constantly boil over with passion in seeking the higher gifts.

And now I will show you a superior way to live that is beyond comparison!ᶜ

---

a 12:28 Most translations render the Greek word *antilēmpsis* (a hapax legomenon) as "helps." However, it is literally "laying hold of (revelation)" or "apprehending (perception)."

b 12:28 This is a hapax legomenon that can be translated "guidance" or "one who steers the ship."

c 12:31 Or "a path corresponding to transcendence."

Thirteen

Love, the Motivation of Our Lives

¹If I were to speak with eloquence in earth's many languages, and in the heavenly tongues of angels,[a] yet I didn't express myself with love,[b] my words would be reduced to the hollow sound of nothing more than a clanging cymbal.

²And if I were to have *the gift of* prophecy[c] with a profound understanding of God's hidden secrets, and if I possessed unending supernatural knowledge, and if I had the greatest gift of faith that could move mountains,[d] but have never learned to love, then I am nothing.

³And if I were to be so generous as to give away everything I owned to feed the poor, and to offer my body to be burned *as a martyr,*[e] without the pure motive of love, I would gain nothing of value.

⁴Love is *large and* incredibly patient.[f] Love is gentle and consistently

---

a 13:1 The implication is that the angels speak a distinct language among themselves that is not known on earth.

b 13:1 The Aramaic word for love is *hooba,* and it is a homonym that also means "to set on fire." It is difficult to fully express the meaning of this word and translate it into English. You could say the Aramaic concept is "burning love" or "fiery love," coming from the inner depths of the heart as an eternal energy, an active power of bonding hearts and lives in secure relationships. The Greek word is *agapē,* which describes the highest form of love. It is the love God has for his people. It is an intense affection that must be demonstrated. It is a loyal, endless, and unconditional commitment of love. Feelings are attached to this love. It is not abstract, but devoted to demonstrating the inward feelings of love toward another with acts of kindness and benevolence.

c 13:2 Or "prophetic powers."

d 13:2 The Greek present infinitive indicates a continuous aspect, which means a faith to keep on removing mountains or to remove one mountain after another.

e 13:3 The Aramaic word used here is a homonym that can mean either "to burn" or "to boast." Because of this, some Greek manuscripts have "I offer my body in order to boast (glory)."

f 13:4 Or "Love patiently endures mistreatment" could mean that love is incredibly patient *even in difficult relationships.* The Aramaic is "Love transforms the spirit."

kind to all. It refuses to be jealous[a] *when blessing comes to someone else.* Love does not brag about one's achievements nor inflate its own importance. [5]Love does not traffic in shame and disrespect, nor selfishly seek its own honor. Love is not easily irritated[b] or quick to take offense.[c] [6]Love joyfully celebrates honesty[d] and finds no delight in what is wrong.[e] [7]Love is a safe place of shelter,[f] for it never stops believing the best for others.[g] Love never takes failure as defeat, for it never gives up.

Perfect Love

[8]Love never stops loving.[h] It extends beyond the gift of prophecy, which eventually fades away.[i] It is more enduring than tongues, which will one day fall silent. Love remains long after *words of* knowledge are forgotten.[j] [9]Our present knowledge and our prophecies are but partial,[k] [10]but when

---

a 13:4 Or "boil with jealousy."

b 13:5 Or "overly sensitive (having sharp edges)."

c 13:5 Or "resentful" or "does not keep score." The Aramaic is "Love does not stare at evil." Love will overlook offenses and remain focused on what is good, refusing to hold resentment in our hearts.

d 13:6 Or "reality (truth)."

e 13:6 Or "injustice" or "unrighteousness."

f 13:7 Or "Love bears all things." Although commonly understood to mean that love can bear hardships of any kind, the nominalized form of the verb (*stego*) is actually the word for "roof" found in Mark 2:4. Paul is saying that love covers all things, like a roof covers the house. See 1 Peter 4:8. Love does not focus on what is wrong but will bear with the shortcomings of others. And like a roof protects and shields, you could say that *love springs no leak.* It is a safe place that offers shelter, not exposure.

g 13:7 Or "It never loses faith."

h 13:8 Or "Love never, not even once, fails (lapses)" or "Love never falls down (It keeps going higher)."

i 13:8 The Aramaic is "Prophecy comes to pass."

j 13:8 That is, the gift of the word of knowledge (1 Corinthians 12:8). Knowledge itself will not pass away or be set aside, for we will learn of God's mercies throughout eternity. This is the gifts of knowledge Paul refers to.

k 13:9 Or "in fragments."

love's perfection arrives, the partial will fade away.[a] [11]When I was a child, I spoke about childish matters, for I saw things like a child and reasoned like a child. But the day came when I matured, and I set aside my childish ways.

[12]For now we see but a faint reflection of riddles and mysteries[b] as though reflected in a mirror, but one day we will see face-to-face.[c] My understanding is incomplete now, but one day I will understand everything, just as everything about me has been fully understood. [13]Until then, there are three things that remain: faith, hope, and love—yet love surpasses them all.[d] So above all else, let love be the beautiful prize for which you run.[e]

---

a 13:8 Perfect love diminishes the importance of prophecy and tongues. Paul could be saying that they will cease being important when compared with perfect love. That which is perfect is love and is greater than the gifts. Perfect love puts everything else in second place, for God is love. See 1 John 4:8, 18. Paul is contrasting spiritual gifts with love, saying, "Gifts will fail, but love will never fail." Like leaves falling to the ground, something greater will one day take their place: the love of God.

b 13:12 The Greek word *ainigma* used here is equal to our English word *enigma*.

c 13:12 Paul is referring to God speaking to Moses "face-to-face" (Hebrew "mouth-to-mouth"), and not using dreams and figures of speech (Numbers 12:8). Transforming love will bring us all face-to-face, mouth-to-mouth with God.

d 13:13 Faith and hope both spring from love, which makes love the greatest virtue of all. Faith and hope are temporary, but love is eternal. Paul gives us ten characteristics of divine love in this chapter. Love: 1) is patient under stress, 2) is kind at all times, 3) is generous, not envious, 4) is humble, not self-promoting, 5) is never rude, 6) does not manipulate by using shame, 7) is not irritable or easily offended, 8) celebrates honesty, 9) does not focus on what is flawed, and 10) is loyal to the end.

e 13:13 Unfortunately, there is a chapter break before this line. Chapter headings are not part of the inspired text. The translator has chosen to insert the partial text of 14:1 here in conclusion to Paul's masterful treatise on love.

Fourteen

Proper Use of Spiritual Gifts

[1]It is good that you are enthusiastic and passionate about spiritual gifts, especially prophecy.[a] [2]When someone speaks in tongues, no one understands a word he says, because he's not speaking to people, but to God—he is speaking intimate mysteries in the Spirit.[b] [3]But when someone prophesies, he speaks to encourage people, to build them up, and to bring them comfort.[c] [4]The one who speaks in tongues advances his own spiritual progress,[d] while the one who prophesies builds up the church. [5]I would be delighted if you all spoke in tongues, but I desire even more that you impart prophetic revelation to others. Greater gain comes through the one who prophesies than the one who speaks in tongues, unless there is interpretation so that it builds up the entire church.

[6]My dear friends, what good is it if I come to you always speaking in tongues? But if I come with a clear revelation from God, or with insight,[e] or with a prophecy, or with a clear teaching, *I can enrich you.*[f] [7]Similarly, if musical instruments, such as flutes or stringed instruments, are out of

---

a 14:1 Or "that you crave spiritual things" or "that you crave spiritual realities."

b 14:2 This verse makes it clear that the tongues Paul refers to are not known languages but Spirit-inspired utterances.

c 14:3 The Greek word *paramythia* (a hapax legomenon) could also be translated "soothing, calming speech" or "affirmation." Paul does not describe prophecy here as predictive, but as influential to advance the spiritual welfare of the body.

d 14:4 See Romans 8:26.

e 14:6 Or "intimate knowledge through experience."

f 14:6 Paul uses these four ministries as examples of what builds up the church. Every congregation needs to focus on all four (revelation from God, insights of truth, prophecy, and teaching), as they are all necessary today.

tune and don't play the arrangement clearly, how will anyone recognize the melody? [8] If the bugle makes a garbled sound, who will recognize the signal to show up for the battle? [9]So it is with you. Unless you speak in a language that's easily understood, how will anyone know what you're talking about? You might as well save your breath!

[10]I suppose that the world has all sorts of languages, and each conveys meaning to the ones who speak it. [11]But I am like a foreigner if I don't understand the language, and the speaker will be like a foreigner to me. [12]And that's what's happening among you. You are so passionate[a] about embracing the manifestations of the Holy Spirit! Now become even more passionate about the things that strengthen the entire church.

[13]So then, if you speak in a tongue, pray for the interpretation to be able to unfold the meaning of what you are saying. [14]For if I am praying in a tongue, my spirit is engaged in prayer but I have no clear understanding of what is being said.

[15]So here's what I've concluded. I will pray in the Spirit, but I will also pray with my mind engaged. I will sing rapturous praises in the Spirit, but I will also sing with my mind engaged. [16]Otherwise, if you are praising God in your spirit, how could someone without the gift participate by adding his "amen" to your giving of thanks, since he doesn't have a clue of what you're saying? [17]Your praise to God is admirable, but it does nothing to strengthen and build up others.

[18]I give thanks to God that I speak in tongues more than all of you, [19]but in the church setting I would rather speak five words that can be understood than ten thousand exotic words in a tongue. That way I could have a role in teaching others.

---

a 14:12 The Greek word implies a boiling over with affection and emotion.

The Function of the Gifts

[20]Beloved ones,[a] don't remain as immature children in your reasoning. As it relates to evil, be like newborns, but in your thinking be mature adults.
[21]For it stands written in the law:

I will bring my message to this people with strange tongues and foreign lips, yet even then they still will not listen to me, says the Lord.[b]

[22]So then, tongues are not a sign for believers, but a miracle for unbelievers. Prophecy, on the other hand, is not for unbelievers, but a miracle sign for believers.

[23]If the entire church comes together and everyone is speaking in tongues, won't the visitors say that you have lost your minds? [24]But if everyone is prophesying, and an unbeliever or one without the gift enters your meeting, he will be convicted by all that he hears and will be called to account, [25]for the intimate secrets of his heart will be brought to light. He will be mystified and fall facedown in worship and say, "God is truly among you!"[c]

Guidelines for Use of the Gifts

[26]Beloved friends,[d] what does all this imply? When you conduct your meetings, you should always let everything be done to build up the church family. Whether you share a song of praise,[e] a teaching, a divine revelation, or a tongue and interpretation, let each one contribute what strengthens others.

---

a 14:20 Or "brothers and sisters."
b 14:21 See Deuteronomy 28:49 and Isaiah 28:11–12.
c 14:25 Or "Truly God is in you."
d 14:26 Or "brothers and sisters."
e 14:26 Or "a psalm."

²⁷If someone speaks in a tongue, it should be two or three,ᵃ one after another, with someone interpreting. ²⁸If there's no one with the interpretation, then he should remain silent in the meeting, content to speak to himself and to God.

²⁹*And the same with prophecy.* Let two or three prophets prophesy and let the other prophets carefully evaluate and discern what is being said. ³⁰But if someone receives a revelation while someone else is still speaking, the one speaking should conclude *and allow the one with fresh revelation the opportunity to share it.*ᵇ ³¹For you can all prophesy in turn and in an environment where all present can be instructed, encouraged, and strengthened. ³²Keep in mind that the anointing to prophesy doesn't mean that the speaker is out of controlᶜ—he can wait his turn.ᵈ ³³For God is the God of harmony, not confusion,ᵉ as is the pattern in all the churches of God's holy believers.

³⁴The womenᶠ should be respectfully silent *during the evaluation of*

---

a 14:27 This could be a Greek idiom (lit., by twos and threes) meaning "just a few."

b 14:30 God wants a fresh word spoken to his people. The churches must allow God's "now" voice to be heard and evaluated by the written Word.

c 14:32 Or "The spirits of the prophets are subject to the prophets." The Aramiac allows for this translation: "The prophecies (spiritual words) of the prophets are subject to the prophets," which could imply that the prophet is to be accountable with his/her prophecies.

d 14:32 From the context it appears that the Corinthians were speaking in tongues and prophesying without regarding others in the body who also had prophetic words to share or a tongue and interpretation. This caused disorder and confusion in the church meetings, with people speaking up and giving their opinions about what was spoken.

e 14:33 Or "instability."

f 14:34 Or "wives."

prophecy in the meetings.[a] They are not allowed to interrupt,[b] but are to be in a support role, as in fact the law teaches.[c] [35]If they want to inquire about something, let them ask their husbands when they get home, for a woman embarrasses herself when she constantly interrupts the church meeting.[d]

[36]Do you actually think that you were the starting point for the Word of God going forth? Were you the only ones it was sent to? *I don't think so!*[e] [37]If anyone considers himself to be a prophet or a spiritual person,[f] let him discern that what I'm writing to you carries the Lord's authority. [38]And if anyone continues not to recognize this, he should not be recognized!

---

a 14:34 Implied in the greater context. The theme Paul is addressing is unity and mutual edification, not simply the role of women. Women are permitted to speak in church, to prophesy, and to minister the gospel. See 1 Corinthians 11:2–16 and 14:31. Paul is apparently prohibiting interrupting the leaders as they evaluate prophetic utterances. It is likely that Paul was addressing a specific issue taking place in the church fellowship of Corinth with women interrupting the meetings with their opinions and questions about the prophetic words just spoken, possibly even words spoken by their husbands.

b 14:34 Or "speak." Interrupting the meeting is implied when compared with 1 Corinthians 11:2–16 and 14:31; Acts 2:16–21 and 21:9.

c 14:34 See Genesis 2:18–24 and 3:16.

d 14:35 One interpretation of this passage is that Paul is quoting from a letter written by the Corinthians to him. They were the ones saying a woman should remain silent and Paul is responding to their questions. In other words, they were imposing a rule in the church that Paul refutes in verse 36. Some manuscripts move verses 34–35 to after verse 40, which causes a few scholars to consider this as evidence of an early introduction into the text by Jewish scribes. The only two places in the New Testament where Paul writes about women being quiet or not teaching in the church are in his letters to the church of Ephesus (1 Timothy) and Corinth. Both cities were centers of worship to the goddess Artemis (Diana), where women had the leading roles of teaching and temple prostitution was commonplace. To the Galatians Paul writes that there is no distinction between believing men and women (Galatians 3:28).

e 14:36 Inferred by the rhetorical question and the disjunctive particle.

f 14:37 Or "a spiritually gifted person."

³⁹So, beloved friends,[a] with all this in mind, be passionate[b] to prophesy and don't forbid anyone from speaking in tongues, ⁴⁰doing all things in a beautiful[c] and orderly way.[d]

Fifteen

The Resurrection of Christ

¹Dear friends,[e] let me give you clearly the heart of the gospel that I've preached to you—the good news that you have heartily received and on which you stand. ²For it is through the revelation of the gospel that you are being saved, if you fasten your life firmly to the message I've taught you, unless you have believed in vain. ³For I have shared with you what I have received and what is of utmost importance:

---

a 14:39 Or "brothers and sisters."

b 14:39 The Greek word zēloō means "a boiling fervor."

c 14:40 Or "respectably." The Aramaic is "with the right design."

d 14:40 This is the Greek word taxis, which can also mean "in battle array." Here are some summary observations concerning believers' gatherings: 1) When the believers gathered, they ate together and frequently observed the Lord's Table. See 1 Corinthians 11:17-33. 2) Men and women participated together and used their spiritual gifts. See 1 Corinthians 11:2–16 and 12. 3) The main purpose of gathering together was the mutual building up and encouragement of one another. See 1 Corinthians 14:1–26. 4) Several people would speak in the meetings, and the leaders would discern and direct. See 1 Corinthians 14:26–40. 5) Expressing love was more important than gifts, teachings, or prophecies. See 1 Corinthians 13. 6) Everything was to be done in a beautiful way and in order. See 1 Corinthians 14:40.

e 15:1 Or "brothers."

The Messiah died for our sins,
fulfilling the prophecies of the Scriptures.
⁴He was buried in a tomb
and was raised from the dead after three days,
as foretold in the Scriptures.ᵃ
⁵Then he appeared to Peter the Rockᵇ
and to the twelve apostles.ᶜ

⁶He also appeared to more than five hundred of his followers at the same time, most of whom are still alive as I write this, though a few have passed away.ᵈ ⁷Then he appeared to Jacobᵉ and to all the apostles. ⁸Last of all he appeared in front of me, like one born prematurely, ripped from the womb.ᶠ ⁹Yes, I am the most insignificant of all the apostles, unworthy even to be called an apostle, because I hunted down believers and persecuted God's church. ¹⁰But God's amazing grace has made me who I am!ᵍ And

---

a 15:4 See Psalm 16:9–10, Luke 24:25–27, and 44–46.

b 15:5 Or "Cephas." Paul includes the bodily appearance of Jesus to his followers as part of the gospel to be believed. What Paul states as the heart of the gospel is: 1) Christ's death, 2) the fulfillment of prophecies, 3) Christ's burial, 4) Christ's resurrection, and 5) Christ supernaturally appeared (manifested) to his followers. More than 515 followers of Jesus saw him after his resurrection, including those mentioned by Paul and Miriam (Mary) at the garden tomb.

c 15:5 Most scholars conclude that verses 3–5 represent an early creed of the apostles on which our Christian faith is based.

d 15 6 Or "Some have fallen asleep," a Hebrew euphemism for death when referring to believers.

e 15:7 See also Galatians 1:19. Jacob was the half-brother of our Lord Jesus. It is unfortunate that other translations of the Bible have substituted James for Jacob. Both Greek and Aramaic leave the Hebrew name as it is, Jacob. At first Jacob did not believe that his brother was the Messiah (John 7:5). Yet after he believed, he wrote what many have come to know as the book of James (or Jacob) and he became the leading elder of the church of Jerusalem (Acts 15:13).

f 15:7 Or "as one born at the wrong time." The Greek word *ektroma* is used to describe a premature birth or miscarriage or abortion. This means Paul's call to be an apostle was not normal; it was sudden and unexpected. Paul never claimed to be part of the Twelve, but an apostle chosen by the resurrected Lord Jesus. See also Ephesians 4:11.

g 15:10 Or "By the grace of God, I am what I am."

his grace to me was not fruitless. In fact, I worked harder than all the rest,[a] yet not in my own strength but God's, for his empowering grace is poured out upon me. [11]So this is what we all have taught you, and whether it was through me or someone else, you have now believed the gospel.

The Importance of the Resurrection

[12]The message we preach is Christ, who has been raised from the dead. So how could any of you possibly say there is no resurrection of the dead? [13]For if there is no such thing as a resurrection from the dead, then not even Christ has been raised.[b] [14]And if Christ has not been raised, all of our preaching has been for nothing and your faith is useless. [15]Moreover, if the dead are not raised, that would mean that we are false witnesses who are misrepresenting God. And that would mean that we have preached a lie, stating that God raised him from the dead, if in reality he didn't.

[16]If the dead aren't raised up,[c] that would mean that Christ has not been raised up either. [17]And if Christ is not alive, you are still lost in your sins and your faith is a fantasy. [18]It would also mean that those believers in Christ who have passed away[d] have simply perished. [19]If the only benefit of our hope in Christ is limited to this life on earth, we deserve to be pitied more than all others![e]

---

a 15:10 See 2 Corinthians 11:16–28.

b 15:13 Paul is showing us that the resurrection of Jesus cannot be separated from the coming resurrection of believers. To remove the truth of Christ's resurrection is to destroy the message of the gospel of hope.

c 15:16 The Aramaic is "if there is no life after death."

d 15:18 Or "those who have fallen asleep in Christ." In the Hebraic mind-set, this is a euphemism for believers who have died.

e 15:19 Why would we be the most pitiable people of all? Because we live a life that contains a measure of hardship and suffering and, at times, possible martyrdom, with no hope of an afterlife. The Aramaic places the emphasis on the apostles who preached the gospel: "If through these (false pretenses) we have preached life eternal through the Messiah, then we (apostles) are the most miserable of all humanity."

[20]But the truth is, Christ is risen from the dead, as the first fruit[a] of a great resurrection harvest of those who have died. [21]For since death came through a man, *Adam*,[b] it is fitting that the resurrection of the dead has also come through a man, *Christ*. [22]Even as all who are in Adam die, so also all who are in Christ will be made alive. [23]But each one in his proper order: Christ, the firstfruits, then those who belong to Christ in his presence.[c]

[24]Then the final stage of completion comes, when he will bring to an end every other rulership, authority, and power, and he will hand over his kingdom to Father God. [25]Until then he is destined to reign[d] *as king* until all hostility has been subdued and placed under his feet.[e] [26]And the last enemy to be subdued and eliminated is death itself.[f]

[27]The Father **has placed all things in subjection under the feet of Christ.**[g] Yet when it says, "all things," it is understood that the Father does not include himself, for he is the one who placed all things in subjection to Christ. [28]However, when everything is subdued and in submission to him, then the Son himself will be subject to the Father, who put all things under his feet.[h] This is so that Father God will be everything in everyone!

Implications of the Resurrection

[29]If there is no resurrection, what do these people think they're doing

---

a 15:20 The first part of the harvest is called the firstfruits. Jesus' resurrection is the first fruit of those who will be raised in resurrection power, never to die again.

b 15:21 See Romans 5:12–21.

c 15:23 Or "appearance (Greek *Parousia*)."

d 15:25 As translated from the Aramaic.

e 15:25 See Psalm 110:1.

f 15:26 See Revelation 20:14.

g 15:27 Or "under his (the Messiah's) feet." See Psalm 8:6.

h 15:28 Christ and the Father are equally one. The work of the Son and the work of the Father may differ, but both will result in all evil being overcome on the earth and the kingdom being given to God.

when they are baptized for the dead? If the dead aren't raised, why be baptized for them?[a] ³⁰And why would we be risking our lives every day?

³¹My brothers and sisters, I continually face death.[b] This is as sure as my boasting of you[c] and our co-union together in the life of our Lord Jesus Christ, who gives me confidence to share my experiences with you. ³²Tell me, why did I fight "wild beasts"[d] in Ephesus if my hope is in this life only? What was the point of that? If the dead do not rise, then

Let's party all night, for tomorrow we die![e]

³³So stop fooling yourselves! Evil companions will corrupt good morals and character.[f] ³⁴Come back to your right senses and awaken to what

---

a 15:29 This is one of the most puzzling verses in all the New Testament. Bible scholars are divided over its meaning, with nearly two hundred interpretations offered. Paul is not condemning nor commending this practice, but merely using it as evidence that the hope of resurrection life after death for the believer is widely believed. Apparently, some believers were baptized in hopes of benefitting those who died before receiving baptism. This practice is not mentioned anywhere else in the Bible nor in other writings of the earliest church fathers.

b 15:31 Some translations render this "I die daily," implying a dying to sin. Yet this is not in the context at all. Paul faces death day by day because of the danger of preaching the gospel in a hostile culture. He is not referring to dying to sin daily, for our death to sin took place on the cross. We died once and for all to sin. See Romans 6:6–11 and Galatians 2:20.

c 15:31 Or "I affirm (swear) by the act of boasting in you." Paul uses a Greek particle that is reserved for taking an oath or swearing to the truth of a statement. This statement by Paul may contain an ellipsis that could be supplied by saying, "I swear by the confidence I have of your salvation *that I am confident also of a coming resurrection.*"

d 15:32 It does not appear that these wild beasts were animals. Rather, Paul is referring figuratively to beastly men and their savage opposition that Paul had to endure in Ephesus (Acts 19:28–31). Elsewhere in the Bible wicked men are called beasts (Titus 1:12; 2 Peter 2:12; Jude 10). The author of Psalm 73 described himself as a "brute beast" when he wandered away from God (Psalm 73:22). When naming all of the hardships that he endured, Paul did not mention fighting wild beasts (2 Corinthians 11:23–28).

e 15:32 See Isaiah 22:13 and Luke 12:19.

f 15:33 This is likely a quotation from the Athenian poet Menander (Thais 218). Paul is using this quote to encourage the believers to stay away from those who deny the resurrection.

is right. Repent from your sinful ways.^a For some have no knowledge of God's wonderful love.^b You should be ashamed that you make me write this way to you!^c

Our Resurrection Body

³⁵I can almost hear someone saying, "How can the dead come back to life? And what kind of body will they have when they are resurrected?" ³⁶Foolish man! Don't you know that what you sow in the ground doesn't germinate unless it dies? ³⁷And what you sow is not the body that will come into being, but the bare seed. And it's hard to tell whether it's wheat or some other seed. ³⁸But when it dies, God gives it a new form, a body to fulfill his purpose, and he sees to it that each seed gets a new body of its own *and becomes the plant he designed it to be.*^d

³⁹All flesh is not identical. Animals have one flesh and human beings another. Birds have their distinct flesh and fish another. ⁴⁰In the same way there are earthly bodies and heavenly bodies. There is a splendor of the celestial body and a different one for the earthly. There is the radiance of the sun and differing radiance for the moon and for the stars. Even the stars differ in their shining. ⁴²And that's how it will be with the resurrection of the dead.

⁴³The body is "sown" in decay, but will be raised in immortality. It is "sown" in humiliation, but will be raised in glorification.^e ⁴⁴It is "sown" in

---

a 15:34 Or "Stop sinning."

b 15:34 As translated from the Aramaic. The Greek is "Some have not the knowledge of God."

c 15:34 The motivation of Paul giving them the exhortation in this verse is the resurrection from the dead. We have a glorious hope of resurrection awaiting us, and for that reason, we live our lives with eternity in view.

d 15:38 Paul is teaching us of the resurrected body every believer will one day possess. Our bodies will then be perfect, renewed, transformed, indestructible, and not limited to the laws of nature. We will never get sick and never experience death again. We will still have our personalities as individuals but without any hint of sin. See Philippians 3:21.

e 15:43 The Aramaic is "They are buried in agony, but raised in glory."

weakness but will be raised in power. If there is a physical body, there is also a spiritual body. [45]For it is written:

The first man, Adam, became a living soul.[a]

The Last Adam[b] became the life-giving Spirit. [46]However, the spiritual didn't come first. The natural precedes the spiritual. [47]The first man was from the dust of the earth; the second Man is the Lord Jehovah,[c] from the realm of heaven.[d] [48]The first one, made from dust, has a race of people just like him, who are also made from dust. The one sent from heaven has a race of heavenly people who are just like him. [49]Once we carried the likeness of the man of dust, but now let us[e] carry the likeness of the Man of heaven.[f]

Transformation

[50]Now, I tell you this, my brothers and sisters, flesh and blood are not able to inherit God's kingdom realm, and neither will that which is decaying be able to inherit what is incorruptible.

[51]Listen, and I will tell you a divine mystery: not all of us will die, but we will all be transformed. [52]It will happen in an instant[g]—in the twinkling of his eye. For when the last trumpet is sounded, the dead will come back

---

a 15:45 See Genesis 2:7.

b 15:45 The Last Adam is Jesus Christ. As the Last Adam, he ended Adam's race and began a new species of humans who are indwelt by the Holy Spirit and carry the life of Christ within them.

c 15:47 As translated from the Aramaic.

d 15:47 In God's eyes there are only two men, Adam and Christ. Every human being is a copy of one or the other. To be in Adam is to be lost and merely human, but to be in Christ is to be wrapped into the Anointed One as one who carries the life of Christ within.

e 15:49 The Aramaic word can be translated either "let us" or "we shall." This may explain the variation among Greek manuscripts.

f 15:49 That is, just as Jesus now has an earthly body transformed into a spiritual body, so we will have our bodies transformed into heavenly bodies.

g 15:52 Or "in an atom of time (Greek *en atomo*)."

to life. We will be indestructible and we will be transformed. [53]For we will discard our mortal "clothes" and slip into a body that is imperishable. What is mortal now will be exchanged for immortality. [54]And when that which is mortal puts on immortality, and what now decays is exchanged for what will never decay, then the Scripture will be fulfilled that says:

Death is swallowed up by a triumphant victory![a]
[55]So death, tell me, where is your victory?
Tell me death, where is your sting?[b]

[56]It is sin that gives death its sting and the law that gives sin its power.[c] [57]But we thank God[d] for giving us the victory as conquerors through our Lord Jesus, the Anointed One.[e] [58]So now, beloved ones,[f] stand firm and secure. Live your lives with an unshakable confidence. We know that we prosper and excel in every season by serving the Lord,[g] because we are assured that our union with the Lord makes our labor productive with fruit that endures.[h]

---

a 15:54 See Isaiah 25:8.

b 15:54 The Aramaic is "your scorpion sting." See Hosea 13:14.

c 15:56 In reading verses 55 and 56 together, we can see that the victory of verse 55 is the total victory over sin at the cross where we were co-crucified with Jesus Christ. The sting of verse 55 that is removed is the empowering of sin by the law.

d 15:57 The Aramaic is "Accept God's grace."

e 15:57 What an amazing summary of what Jesus Christ has accomplished for us! Although Satan seemed to be victorious, the cross of Christ defeated him, defeated death, and defeated sin, making us into victorious conquerors who have hope beyond the grave.

f 15:58 Or "dear brothers and sisters."

g 15:58 As translated from the Aramaic. The Greek can be translated "Always have the Lord's possessions in abundance."

h 15:58 Or "Your labor in the Lord is not without effect." This final clause is litotes, a double negative, which is best conveyed in a positive form.

Sixteen

An Offering for Believers in Jerusalem

¹Now, concerning the collection I want you to take for God's holy believers *in Jerusalem who are in need,*ᵃ I want you to follow the same instructions I gave the churches of Galatia.ᵇ ²Every Sunday, each of you make a generous offering by taking a portion of whatever God has blessed you with and place it in safekeeping. Then I won't have to make a special appeal when I come. ³ When I arrive, I will send your gift to the poor in Jerusalem along with a letter of explanation, carried by those whom you approve. ⁴If it seems advisable for me to accompany them, I'll be glad to have them travel with me.

Paul's Plans to Visit Corinth

⁵I plan to be traveling through Macedonia, and afterward I will visit you ⁶and perhaps stay there for a while, or even spend the winter with you. Afterward you can send me on my journey, wherever I go next, with your financial support. ⁷For it's not my desire to just see you in passing, but I would like to spend some time with you if the Lord permits. ⁸Regardless, I will remain in Ephesus until *the feast of* Pentecost. ⁹There's an amazing door of opportunity standing wide open for me to minister here, even though there are many who oppose and stand against me.ᶜ

¹⁰When Timothy arrives, make sure that he feels at home while he's

---

a 16:1 Although it is implied here, it is made explicit in verse 3 that the offering was for those in Jerusalem.

b 16:1 Galatia is a region of the Anatolia province of central Turkey.

c 16:9 See Acts 19.

with you, for he's advancing the Lord's work just as I am. [11]Don't let anyone disparage or look down on him, but kindly help him on his way with financial support so that he may come back to me, for I am waiting for him and the brothers to return.

[12]Now, about our brother Apollos. I've tried hard to convince him to come visit you with the other brothers,[a] but it's simply not the right time for him now. But *don't worry*, he'll come when he has the opportunity.

Paul's Final Instructions and Greetings

[13]Remember to stay alert and hold firmly to all that you believe. Be mighty and full of courage. [14]Let love and kindness be the motivation behind all that you do. [15]Dear brothers and sisters, I have a request to make of you. Give special recognition to Stephanas and his family, for they were the first converts in Achaia,[b] and they have fully devoted themselves to serve God's holy people.[c] [16]I urge you to honor and support them, and all those like them who work so diligently for the Lord.

[17]I was delighted when Stephanas,[d] Fortunatus,[e] and Achaicus[f] arrived, for they've made up for your absence. [18]They have refreshed my spirit in the same way they've refreshed yours. Be sure to honor people like this.

---

a 16:12 The other brothers may have been those who carried the letter from the Corinthians to Paul, Stephanas, Fortunatus, and Achaicus (1 Corinthians 16:17).

b 16:15 At the time Paul wrote to the Corinthians, Achaia was a Roman province in southern Greece.

c 16:15 Whenever we minister to God's people, we are ministering to the Lord. See Matthew 25:34–46.

d 16:17 Stephanas means "crowned." Some believe that he was the Philippian jailor who, along with his household, became the first believers in Philippi.

e 16:17 Fortunatus means "blessed." He is recognized in the Orthodox Church as one of the seventy disciples sent out by Jesus as an apostle.

f 16:17 Achaicus means "a native of Achaia." He is recognized in church history as one of the seventy disciples sent out by Jesus as an apostle.

¹⁹All the churches of western Turkey*a* send their loving greetings to you. Aquila and Prisca*b* greet you warmly in the Lord with those of their house church. ²⁰All of your fellow believers *here in Ephesus* send their greetings. Greet one another with a sacred kiss.*c*

²¹In my own handwriting, I, Paul, add my loving greeting.

²²If anyone doesn't sincerely love the Lord, he deserves to be doomed as an outcast.*d* Our Lord has come!*e* ²³May the grace and favor of our Lord Jesus be with you. ²⁴I send my love to all who are joined in the life of Jesus, the Anointed One.

---

a 16:19 Or "(the Roman province) of Asia."

b 16:19 Prisca was a diminutive form of Priscilla ("long life"). She and her husband, Aquila ("eagle"), were tentmakers like Paul. They were not only business partners but partners with him in ministry. See Acts 18:2, 18, and 26, and 2 Timothy 4:19.

c 16:20 What makes a kiss holy is that it comes from the love of God. See Song of Songs 1:2.

d 16:22 Or "accursed."

e 16:22 Or "Maranatha!" This is an Aramaic word that can be translated in two ways, "Come, our Lord" or "Our Lord has come."

2 Corinthians

Translator's Introduction to 2 Corinthians

AT A GLANCE

Author: The Apostle Paul

Audience: The Church of Corinth

Date: AD 56–57

Type of Literature: A letter

Major Themes: The person and work of Jesus, the gospel, the new covenant, Paul's apostolic ministry, Christian living, and generosity

Outline:

Letter Opening — 1:1–11
Paul's Rift with the Corinthians — 1:12–2:13
Paul's Apostolic Ministry — 2:14–7:16
Paul's Collection Effort — 8:1–9:15
Paul's Ministry Defense — 10:1–18
Paul Speaks as a Fool — 11:1–12:10
Paul's Final Warning — 12:11–13:13

ABOUT 2 CORINTHIANS

You are about to read a book written by a man who suffered for the cause of Christ, a man who knew trouble and how to overcome in victory. In 2 Corinthians you'll find a letter written by an apostle to a church that he planted—a church that was in need of a father's advice. In many ways, this letter serves as an apostolic manual for the body of Christ, replete with supernatural encounters, glory, love, and truth. This book is full of spiritual encouragement and revelation!

The church of Corinth had already received at least two prior letters from Paul. What we have in our New Testament as 1 Corinthians was Paul's second letter, making 2 Corinthians his third. The church had received Paul's rebuke in his prior letters, and now they were tender, open, and ready to receive all that their spiritual father had to impart. Although influenced by those who had claimed to be "super-apostles," their hearts were bound in love to Paul and the grace of God that was upon him.

How the church today needs the truth and love from this anointed apostle! As you read, picture yourself in the congregation in Corinth, hearing the letter read publicly. Let its truth penetrate your heart and stir you, as a new creation, to a greater passion to follow Jesus. Here you will find the wonderful secrets Paul learned about how to turn troubles into triumph. May you find more than you expected as you read through 2 Corinthians. Enjoy!

PURPOSE

Paul's letter to the church of Corinth is one of his most personal letters. In it, he wrote to defend his apostleship in the face of rival "super-apostles," as he called them, who were threatening the spiritual ground Paul had so carefully, paternally tilled. In defending his ministry Paul wrote to address a deeper issue with the Corinthian believers. He clarified how the gospel should impact every ounce of their lives, encouraging them to stay faithful to the truth and love that had been deposited in their hearts.

One truth the Corinthians had not yet grasped, which informed the purpose behind this letter, was their inability to fully embrace the scandal of the cross. The glory of the cross is the glory of the one who was crucified upon it. They had neglected to appreciate the self-suffering nature of the cross-centered life. So Paul passionately pointed to the glory that lies ahead, especially in the midst of weakness and suffering, stirring them to keep their eyes on the prize. What wonderful insights fill the pages of this letter, magnifying the majesty of Christ, which shatters the darkness, reconciles the lost, and recreates us anew!

AUTHOR AND AUDIENCE

Paul wrote this letter to a needy congregation in the Roman city of Corinth to bring them comfort, wisdom, and insight. Many believe that this letter is actually a compilation of two: a so-called "tearful" letter that makes up the ending (chapters 10–13), which was possibly sent before the main "reconciliation" letter (chapters 1–9). Apparently, a number of people had infiltrated the church of Corinth and challenged Paul's apostolic credentials and the gospel he preached, which had bearing on what they believed.

In this letter, we get a glimpse into Paul's own trials and the path of continual triumph that he discovered. He opens his heart to us in this book, sharing his deep emotions, perhaps more here than in any of his other writings. We learn of the magnitude of his sufferings as he informs us of the trials he experienced, which informed his understanding of the gospel. As a minister of reconciliation, Paul brings tremendous energy to the church through his letters. He is a true hero of the faith!

MAJOR THEMES

The Incarnation and Crucifixion of Christ. One of the major themes of this letter is the incarnate presence of Christ on earth. As Paul wrote, "Although he was infinitely rich, he impoverished himself for your sakes" (8:9). Christ's coming and condescension to our lives reveals his "meekness and gentleness" (10:1), but Christ is also clearly God (1:2). Christ's incarnation wasn't for nothing; there was a purpose to his impoverishment.

The Son of God came to earth "so that by his poverty, you could become rich beyond measure" (8:9). Jesus, who knew no sin, became sin for us, "so that we, *who did not know righteousness*, might become the righteousness of God through our union with him" (5:21). He was "crucified as a 'weakling,'" (13:4) yet he "now lives again" (5:15). Because he was, and because he does, "All that is related to the old order has vanished. Behold, everything is fresh and new" (5:17).

The Call of the Gospel. One of the clearest descriptions of the gospel's call on our lives is found in 5:18, "God has made all things new and reconciled us to himself." Paul opens up the mystery of our being made right with God through the finished work of Christ on the cross. This call has gone out from God into the hearts of all his lovers: "Turn back to God and be reconciled to him!" (5:21).

This gospel call is also heard in and through the ministry that God has entrusted to us, "the ministry of opening the door of reconciliation to God" (5:19). Amazingly, we are all "ambassadors of the Anointed One who carry the message of Christ to the world" (5:20). Through our words and deeds, it's "as though God were tenderly pleading with them directly through our lips" (5:20). Our motivation is to honor God and love Christ, while petitioning people on Christ's behalf to turn back to God and be made new.

Christian Ministry. This letter is one of Paul's most personal, because in it he exhibits the characteristics of a spiritual father who has been entrusted by God as a caretaker of his children. From the beginning he roots the compassion and comfort he passes along to others in God himself (1:3). His generosity as a laborer on behalf of the Corinthians flows from God's own generous hand (chapters 8–9). Paul is paternally devoted to his children, so much so that he feels their weaknesses and burns with zeal for their restoration (11:29). Like all parents, Paul's affection was clear: he was willing to "gladly spend all that I have and all that I am for you" (12:15). In many ways Paul outlines a theology of pastoral service that should be modeled and adopted by all ministers of the gospel.

The Christian Life. At the center of Paul's letter is a strong call to live a life of holiness; the Christian life is a holy life. He tells us not to "team up with unbelievers in mismatched alliances" (6:14). Which doesn't mean that we are to avoid befriending the world, but to avoid living like the world. We are to "come out from among them and be separate" (6:17). Holy living is deliberate living, for as Christians, we are called to "remove everything from our lives that contaminates body and spirit" and develop holiness within us (7:1).

Another aspect of the Christian life Paul addresses is the paradox of our Christian existence. We are comforted, yet afflicted; we are secure, yet we suffer; we are both strong and weak; we experience joy and sorrow; we die yet live. God "comes alongside of us to comfort us in every suffering" (1:4). When we are at our weakest, we "sense more deeply the mighty power of Christ living in me" (12:9). And though "we continually share in the death of Jesus," his "resurrection life...will be revealed through our humanity" (4:10).

Christian Generosity. One aspect of Christian living that Paul highlighted is that of generosity. During his apostolic ministry, Paul spent a good amount of energy over the course of five years collecting resources for "the poor among the holy believers in Jerusalem" (Romans 15:26). In this letter Paul made one more appeal to the church of Corinth. He attempted to stir them to greater love by issuing a challenge of generous giving. He compared Christian generosity to the "extravagant grace of our Lord Jesus Christ" (8:9). It is an "act of worship" (8:11) and maintains "a fair balance" (8:14) between believers. Christian generosity should "flow from your heart—not from a sense of religious duty" (9:7) and should be marked by "enthusiasm" and "joy," because "God loves hilarious generosity" (9:7).

One

Paul's Greeting

[1]From Paul to God's called ones, his church in Corinth.

I have been chosen by Jesus Christ to be his apostle according to God's perfect plan. Our brother Timothy joins me in writing to you and all the holy believers throughout the Roman province of Achaia.[a] [2]May undeserved favor and endless peace be yours continually from our Father God and from our Lord Jesus, the Anointed One!

[3]All praises belong to the God and Father of our Lord Jesus Christ. For he is the Father of tender mercy and the God of endless comfort.[b] [4]He always comes alongside us to comfort us in every suffering so that we can come alongside those who are in any painful trial. We can bring them this same comfort that God has poured out upon us. [5]And just as we experience the abundance of Christ's own sufferings,[c] even more of God's comfort will cascade upon us through our union with Christ.

[6]If troubles weigh us down, that just means that we will receive even more comfort to pass on to you for your deliverance! For the comfort pouring into us empowers us to bring comfort to you. And with this comfort upholding you, you can endure *victoriously* the same suffering that

---

a 1:2 Although this letter was addressed primarily to the Corinthians, it was intended to be read by the churches in southern Greece (Achaia).

b 1:3 Unlike Paul's other letters, he skips over making his customary pleasant greeting to the Corinthians and begins this letter bursting with exuberant praise to God, who had delivered him from all of his painful ordeals. Tender mercy and compassion originate with God. As a kind father has compassion on his children, so God tenderly cares for each one of us. When suffering greets us, the God of mercy sustains us. His comfort is permanent and endless. See Micah 7:18–19.

c 1:5 That is, "the sufferings we endure because of faithfully following Christ."

we experience. [7]Now our hope for you is unshakable,[a] because we know that just as you share in our sufferings you will also share in God's comforting strength.

[8]Brothers and sisters, you need to know about the severe trials we experienced while we were in western Turkey.[b] All of the hardships we passed through crushed us beyond our ability to endure, and we were so completely overwhelmed that we were about to give up entirely.[c] [9]It felt like we[d] had a death sentence written upon our hearts, *and we still feel it to this day*. It has taught us to lose all faith in ourselves and to place all of our trust in the God who raises the dead. [10]He has rescued us from terrifying encounters with death. And now we fasten our hopes on him to continue to deliver us from death yet again, [11]as you labor together with us through prayer.[e] *Because there are so many interceding for us*, our deliverance will cause even more people to give thanks to God. What a gracious gift of mercy surrounds us because of your prayers!

Apostolic Integrity

[12]We rejoice in saying with complete honesty and a clear conscience[f] that God has empowered us to conduct ourselves[g] in a holy manner and

---

a 1:7 Or "firmly guaranteed."

b 1:8 Or "Asia." This was not the continent of Asia known today, but the Roman province of Asia comprised of western Turkey.

c 1:8 We are not told exactly what overwhelming suffering Paul endured that caused him to write these words with such honest emotion. Some believe he had escaped an assassination attempt or perhaps a mob who had gathered to kill him. Regardless, the sufferings Paul endured were many. See 2 Corinthians 11:23–33.

d 1:9 The Greek text is extremely emphatic: "It felt like we ourselves, within our very beings, had received the verdict of death!"

e 1:11 Or "as you lift up your faces to God in prayer." Paul knew that intercessory prayer has the power to change the future.

f 1:12 Or "indeed, our boasting and the testimony of our conscience."

g 1:12 Paul regularly uses "we" and "our" in 2 Corinthians to refer to apostles and apostolic ministry.

with no hidden agenda.[a] God's marvelous grace enables us to minister to everyone with pure motives, not in the clever wisdom of the world. This is especially true in all of our dealings with you. [13]We write to you with words that are clearly understood, and there is no need for you to try to read between the lines of what we write in hopes that you can completely and accurately understand *our hearts*. [14]We know you have already understood us in a measure and that you will eventually come to understand us fully.[b] Then you'll be able to boast of us even as we will boast of you in the day of our Lord Jesus.

Paul Explains His Changed Plans

[15-16]With this confidence, I'm wanting to visit you before and after my trip to Macedonia[c] so that you enjoy a second experience of grace.[d] Afterward, I'm hoping you will be able to aid me on my journey to Israel.[e] [17]When I revised my itinerary, was I vacillating? Or do I make my plans with unprincipled motives,[f] ready to flip-flop with a "yes" and a "no" in

---

a 1:12 Or "We have behaved in the world with holiness and godly sincerity (Aramaic, purity)." Our boast and joy in ministry is not what we have done or how many followers we have, but that our conscience is clean and our motives unmixed. Paul is not taking credit for himself but stating clearly that God's grace was his source of strength and purity.

b 1:14 Or "to the end."

c 1:15 Implied and made explicit from verse 15.

d 1:15 Or "a second pleasure." It is possible Paul is using a figure of speech for his second trip to visit them.

e 1:16 Or "Judea."

f 1:17 Or "according to the (ways of the) flesh."

the same breath? *Of course not!*[a] [18]For as God is true to his word, my promise[b] to you was not a *fickle* "yes" when I meant "no."

[19]Jesus Christ is the Son of God, and he is the one whom Timothy, Silas, and I have preached to you—and he has never been both a "yes" and a "no." He has always been and always will be for us a resounding "YES!" [20]For all of God's promises find their "yes" of fulfillment in him.[c] And as his "yes" and our "amen"[d] ascend to God, we bring him glory![e]

[21]Now, it is God himself who has anointed us. And he is constantly strengthening both you and us in union with Christ. [22]*He knows we are his* since he has also stamped his seal of love[f] over our hearts and has

---

a 1:17 The change of Paul's plans was used by his detractors as a sign of him being untrustworthy. But Paul explains that his itinerary change was not an indication of a lack of concern for them, but because he didn't want to come and have to rebuke them. He wanted to give the Holy Spirit time in their lives to help work out their issues. His longing was to come with joy and to impart his joy to them, rather than causing more pain. This is why he wrote an emotional letter to them pleading with them to change their ways.

b 1:18 Or "my message."

c 1:20 The Aramaic can be translated "All of the kingdoms of God are in him."

d 1:20 The Hebrew word for *amen* means "That's right!"

e 1:20 This elliptical sentence could imply: 1) It is through Christ that we hear and believe God's promises and say the declaration of our faith, "Amen," or 2) it is Christ who speaks through us the "Amen (of faith)."

f 1:21 The Greek word for seal is *sphragizō*. God has sealed believers with a seven-fold seal: 1) a seal of security, sealed tightly and kept secure in God's love (Deuteronomy 32:34; Job 14:17; Mattnew27:66), 2) a seal of authentication that marks us as God's very own (1 Kings 21:8; Esther 8:10; John 6:27), 3) a seal to certify genuineness (Esther 8:8, 10; John 3:33), 4) a seal of ownership (Nehemiah 10:1; Jeremiah 32:44; 2 Corinthians 1:22), 5) a seal of approval (Ephesians 1:13–14), 6) a seal of righteousness (Romans 4:11), and 7) a seal denoting a promise to be fulfilled (Ephesians 1:13–14; 4:30; 2 Corinthians 5:5). The "mark" given by the "beast" is upon the forehead and hand, but the "seal" of Christ is over our hearts. Jesus, our Bridegroom, invites us to place him over our hearts like a fiery seal of love, the jealous flame of God that burns continually in our hearts (Song of Songs 8:6). We are born of the Spirit, sealed with the Spirit, indwelt by the Spirit, baptized in the Spirit, filled with the Spirit, made one (unity) in the Spirit, given gifts of the Spirit, and given ministries by the Spirit. He is a promise, a seal, and a guarantee of receiving our full inheritance. The Greek word for down payment is *arrabōn* and is used in Greek culture for "engagement ring." Notice in verses 21–22 that the Trinity (Father, Son, and Holy Spirit) is involved in bringing all this to pass.

given us the Holy Spirit like an engagement ring is given to a bride—a down payment of the blessings to come!

A Change in Paul's Travel Plans

²³Now, I call upon this faithful God as a witness against me *if I'm not telling you the absolute truth.* It was because I hold you in my heart that I decided not to return to Corinth, in order to spare you *the humiliation of my rebuke.* ²⁴But I don't want to imply that *as leaders* we coerce you or somehow want to rule over your faith.ᵃ Instead, we are your partners who are called to increase your joy.ᵇ And we know that you already stand firm because of your *strong* faith.ᶜ

Two

Paul's Previous Letter

¹So *until these issues were settled,*ᵈ I decided against paying you another painful visit.ᵉ ²For if I brought you pain, you would be unable to bring me joy. ³And this was the very point I made in my letter, for I didn't want to come and find sadness filling the very ones who should give me cheer.

---

a 1:24 Or "dictate what you must believe."

b 1:24 The Aramaic is "We are helpers of your joy." True ministry in God's kingdom is to be coworkers with those we serve, laboring to see them overflow with joy. There is no control that leaders are to have over the people they serve; rather, they are to inspire lives to be filled with the joy of knowing Jesus.

c 1:24 The Aramaic can be translated "For it is through faith that you stand."

d 2:1 See 2 Corinthians 2:4–11.

e 2:1 Paul implies that he had already paid them one painful visit (1:15–17).

But I'm confident *that you will do what's right* so that my joyous delight will be yours.

⁴I wrote you previously sobbing and with a broken heart.ᵃ I was filled with anguish and deep distress. I had no intention of causing you pain but to convey the overwhelming measure of my love for you. ⁵For the one who has caused me grief has not only grieved me but, to some extent, has caused you all grief as well. ⁶I believe that your united rebukeᵇ has been punishment enough for him. ⁷Instead of more punishment, what he needs most is your encouragement through your gracious display of forgiveness. ⁸I beg you to reaffirm your deep love for him.

⁹You see, I wrote previously in order to see if your hearts would pass the test and if you were willing to follow my counsel in everything. ¹⁰If you freely forgive anyone for anything, then I also forgive him. And if I have forgiven anything, I did so for you before the face of Christ, ¹¹so that we would not be exploitedᶜ by the adversary, Satan, for we know his clever schemes.

¹²When I arrived at Troas, bringing the wonderful news of Christ, the Lord opened a great door of opportunity to minister there. ¹³Still, I had no peace of mind, because I couldn't find my dear brother Titusᵈ anywhere. So after saying good-bye to the believers, I set out for Macedonia to look for him.

---

a 2:4 Paul is referring here (and in 2:3) not to 1 Corinthians but to a letter he had written them after they received 1 Corinthians and failed to properly respond to what he wrote. This painful letter (see also 7:8) was a reprimand that powerfully impacted them. God has sovereignly chosen that we would not have this "painful letter" included in the New Testament, but its impact on the Corinthians is noteworthy. See also Proverbs 27:6.

b 2:6 The Aramaic can be translated "Your triple rebuke is enough punishment."

c 2:11 The Aramaic is "so that Satan will not overtake us."

d 2:13 Titus was a spiritual son to Paul whom he greatly loved. This is the Titus Paul wrote his letter to (book of Titus). He was responsible to collect and distribute an offering for the church in Jerusalem (2 Corinthians 8:6). It is possible that Titus was the one who carried the "painful letter" to Corinth. After finding Titus in Macedonia, Paul sent him back to Corinth to deliver this letter (2 Corinthians).

Apostolic Ministry

[14]God always makes his grace visible[a] in Christ, who includes us as partners of his endless triumph.[b] Through our yielded lives he spreads[c] the fragrance of the knowledge of God everywhere we go. [15]We[d] have become the unmistakable aroma *of the victory* of the Anointed One to God[e]—a perfume of life to those being saved and the odor of death[f] to those who are perishing. [16]The unbelievers smell a deadly stench that leads to death, but believers smell the life-giving aroma that leads to abundant life. And who of us can rise to this challenge?[g] [17]For unlike so many, we are not peddlers[h] of God's Word who water down the message. We are those sent from God with pure motives, who speak in the sight of God[i] from our union with Christ.

---

a 2:14 As translated from the Aramaic. The Greek is "Thanks be to God."

b 2:14 Or "who always leads us as captives in his triumphant procession." This difficult-to-translate passage may be an allusion to the Roman victory procession in celebration of their military triumphs. See also Colossians 2:15.

c 2:14 Or "manifests."

d 2:15 Although this is true of every believer, Paul, throughout this section, uses "we" in reference to apostles.

e 2:15 Or "We are Christ's sweet fragrance (of sacrifice) that ascends to God."

f 2:15 That is, a sacrifice ready to be offered.

g 2:16 As challenging as our ministry may be, God empowers us to overcome by his Holy Spirit. He empowers everyone he calls.

h 2:17 The Greek word kapēleuō (a hapax legomenon) means "retailer," but in classical Greek it comes with a negative connotation ("one who sells at an illegitimate profit"). The adverbial form of the noun is "cheating" or "deceitful."

i 2:17 Paul states that his ministry of teaching and preaching happened while he was in the presence of God. His eyes were set on God, not on the people's response.

Three

Servants of the New Covenant

[1]Are we beginning to sound like those who speak highly of themselves? Do you really need letters of recommendation *to validate our ministry,* like others do?[a] Do we really need your letter of endorsement? *Of course not!* [2]For your very lives are our "letters of recommendation," permanently engraved on our hearts, recognized and read by everybody. [3]As a result of our ministry, you are living letters written by Christ, not with ink but by the Spirit of the Living God—not carved onto stone tablets[b] but on the tablets of tender hearts. [4]We carry this confidence in our hearts because of our union with Christ before God. [5]Yet we don't see ourselves as capable enough to do anything in our own strength, for our true competence flows from God's *empowering presence.* [6]He alone makes us adequate ministers who are focused on an entirely new covenant. Our ministry is not based on the letter of the law but through the *power of the Spirit.* The letter of the law kills, but the Spirit pours out life.[c]

The Glorious Ministry of the Spirit

[7]Even the ministry that was characterized by chiseled letters on stone tablets came with a dazzling measure of glory, though it produced

---

a 3:1 Apparently, there were some insecure and phony ministers who would carry forged letters of recommendation in an attempt to validate their ministry. Paul's supernatural ministry needed no such letter of recommendation.

b 3:3 See Exodus 24:12; 31:18; 34:1; Deuteronomy 9:10–11; Jeremiah 38:33 (LXX).

c 3:6 To illustrate this, on the day when the law was given by Moses, three thousand people were killed, but on the day the Spirit was poured out at Pentecost, three thousand people received new life. See Exodus 32:28 and Acts 2:41.

death. The Israelites couldn't bear to gaze on the glowing face of Moses[a] because of the radiant splendor shining from his countenance—a glory destined to fade away.

[8]Yet how much more radiant is this new and glorious ministry of the Spirit *that shines from us!* [9]For if the former ministry of condemnation was ushered in with a measure of glory, how much more does the ministry that imparts righteousness far excel in glory.[b] [10]What once was glorious no longer holds any glory because of the increasingly[c] greater glory that has replaced it. [11]The fading ministry came with a portion of glory, but now we embrace the unfading ministry of a permanent impartation of glory. [12]So then, with this amazing hope living in us, we step out in freedom and boldness to speak the truth.

[13]We are not like Moses, who used a veil to hide the glory to keep the Israelites from staring at him as it faded away.[d] [14]Their minds were closed and hardened, for even to this day that same veil comes over their minds when they hear the words of the former covenant. The veil has not yet been lifted from them, for it is only eliminated when one is joined to the Messiah. [15]So until now, whenever the Old Testament[e] is being read, the same blinding comes over their hearts. [16]But the moment one turns to the Lord[f] with an open heart, the veil is lifted *and they see.*[g] [17]Now, the "Lord" *I'm referring to* is the Holy Spirit,[h] and wherever he is Lord, there is freedom.

---

a 3:7 See Exodus 34:29.

b 3:9 The contrast here is between a ministry that brings awareness of sin and leads to condemnation and a new ministry that confirms to us that we are made righteous and innocent by the work of the cross and the grace of the Spirit.

c 3:10 As translated from the Aramaic and implied contextually in the Greek.

d 3:13 Or "the end of what was fading."

e 3:15 Or "Moses," an obvious metonymy.

f 3:16 The Aramaic is "Lord Yahweh."

g 3:16 See Exodus 34:34.

h 3:17 Paul is teaching us that not every time the word *Lord* appears does it mean Jesus Christ. Here we see that "the Lord" refers to the Holy Spirit. When the Holy Spirit is ruling, speaking, convincing us of truth, there is freedom. Jesus calls the Holy Spirit the

[18]We can all draw close to him with the veil removed from our faces. And with no veil we all become like mirrors who brightly reflect the glory of the Lord *Jesus.*[a] We are being transfigured[b] into his very image as we move from one brighter level of glory to another.[c] And this glorious transfiguration comes from the Lord, who is the Spirit.[d]

Four

New Covenant Ministry

[1]Now, it's because of God's mercy[e] that we have been entrusted with the privilege of this *new covenant* ministry. And we will not quit or faint with weariness. [2]We reject every shameful cover-up and refuse to resort

---

Lord of the harvest who prepares the workers and the harvest fields, sending them out into specific places for the reaping of souls. See Matthew 9:38.

a 3:18 Or "We all, with unveiled faces, behold the glory of the Lord as in a mirror."

b 3:18 The Greek verb *metamorphoō* is the same word used for Jesus' being transfigured on the mountain (Matthew 17:2; Mark 9:2) and for our transfiguration through the renewing of the thoughts of our minds (Romans 12:2).

c 3:18 The source of our transformation comes from Christ's glory, and the destination we are brought to is more glory. The transforming glory is the result of gazing upon the beauty and splendor of Jesus Christ.

d 3:18 Notice the ten aspects of New Testament ministry given by Paul: 1) It is based on the triumph of Christ over every power of darkness (2:14), 2) It diffuses the fragrant aroma of Christ everywhere (2:15–16), 3) It refuses to water down the Word of God (2:17), 4) It produces living letters of Christ (3:3), 5) It is not based on the clever abilities of men but God's empowering presence (3:6), 6) It imparts life (3:6), 7) It flows from the Holy Spirit (3:8, 17–18), 8) It imparts righteousness (3:9), 9) It contains a greater glory than the law (3:10–11), and 10) It brings the transfiguration of believers into greater levels of glory (3:18).

e 4:1 Or "God has mercied us." The Aramaic is "God's mercy rests on us."

to cunning trickery or distorting the Word of God.[a] Instead, we open up our souls to you[b] by presenting the truth to everyone's conscience in the sight and presence of God. ³Even if our gospel message is veiled, it is only veiled to those who are perishing, ⁴for their minds have been blinded by the god of this age,[c] leaving them in unbelief. Their blindness keeps them from seeing the dayspring light[d] of the wonderful news of the glory of Jesus Christ, who is the *divine* image of God.

⁵We don't preach ourselves, but rather the lordship of Jesus Christ, for we are your servants for Jesus' sake. ⁶For God, who said, **"Let brilliant light shine out of darkness,"**[e] is the one who has cascaded his light into us—the brilliant dawning light of the glorious knowledge of God as we gaze into the face of Jesus Christ.[f]

Treasure in Clay Jars

⁷We are like common clay jars that carry this glorious treasure within, so that the extraordinary overflow of power will be seen as God's, not ours.[g] ⁸Though we experience every kind of pressure, we're not crushed. At times we don't know what to do, but quitting is not an option.[h] ⁹We are

---

a 4:2 Or "handle the word of God dishonestly."

b 4:2 As translated from the Aramaic. The Greek is "we commend ourselves."

c 4:4 Satan is called the god of this age. He uses trickery, deceit, accusation, and slander to blind people's hearts. See John 8:44; 12:31; 14:30; Ephesians 2:2.

d 4:4 The Aramaic is "the flame of the good news."

e 4:6 Paul helps us to understand that "light" is both literal and a metaphor for spiritual revelation, and shows that the creation narrative provides us with an allegory pointing to the experience of new birth in Christ. See Genesis 1:3 and Isaiah 9:2.

f 4:6 Or "in the face-to-face presence of Christ."

g 4:7 This verse begins a long and complicated Greek sentence that ends with verse 10. Paul uses figurative language to say that we are common clay jars (created from dust/clay) yet we possess the brilliant light of God's glory, Jesus Christ, and carry him as treasure in our being. The outward vessel is not as important as the glorious treasure within. The metaphors here may allude to Gideon's clay pots that had burning torches inside (Judges 7:16).

h 4:8 Or "perplexed but not thoroughly perplexed." The Aramaic can be translated "We are corrected but not condemned."

persecuted by others, but God has not forsaken us. We may be knocked down, but not out. [10]We continually share in the death of Jesus in our own bodies[a] so that the resurrection life of Jesus will be revealed through our humanity. [11]We consider living to mean that we are constantly being handed over to death for Jesus' sake so that the life of Jesus will be revealed through our humanity. [12]So, then, death is at work in us but it releases life in you.

[13]We have the same Spirit of faith that is described in the Scriptures when it says, **"First I believed, then I spoke in faith."**[b] So we also first believe then speak in faith. [14]We do this because we are convinced that he who raised Jesus will raise us up with him, and together we will all be brought into his presence. [15]Yes, all things work for your enrichment[c] so that more of God's marvelous grace will spread to more and more people, resulting in an even greater increase of praise[d] to God, bringing him even more glory!

[16]So no wonder we don't give up. For even though our outer person gradually wears out, our inner being is renewed every single day. [17]We view our slight, short-lived troubles in the light of eternity. We see our difficulties as the substance that produces for us an eternal, weighty glory far beyond all comparison, [18]because we don't focus our attention on what is seen but on what is unseen. For what is seen is temporary, but the unseen realm is eternal.

---

a 4:10 Or "carry about in the body the death of Jesus."
b 4:13 See Psalm 116:10.
c 4:15 See Romans 8:28.
d 4:15 Or "to cause thanksgiving to super-abound."

Five

Living by Faith

[1]We are convinced that even if these bodies we live in are folded up at death like tents, we will still have a God-built home that no human hands have built, which will last forever in the heavenly realm. [2]We inwardly sigh[a] *as we live in these physical "tents,"* longing to put on a new body for our life in heaven, [3]in the belief that once we put on our new "clothing" we won't find ourselves "naked." [4]So, while living in this "tent," we groan under its burden, not because we want to die but because we want these new bodies. We crave for all that is mortal to be swallowed up by *eternal life.* [5]*And this is no empty hope,* for God himself is the one who has prepared us for this wonderful destiny. And to confirm this promise, he has given us the Holy Spirit, like an engagement ring, as a guarantee.[b]

[6]That's why we're always full of courage. Even while we're at home in the body, we're homesick to be with the Master—[7]for we live by faith, not by what we see with our eyes. [8]We live with a joyful confidence, yet at the same time we take delight in the thought of leaving our bodies behind to be at home with the Lord. [9]So whether we live or die[c] we make it our life's passion[d] to live our lives pleasing to him.[e] [10]For one day we will all be openly revealed before Christ on his throne[f] so that each of us

---

a 5:2 The Aramaic uses the phrase "to sigh and yearn."

b 5:5 By giving us the Holy Spirit, God is making us a promise, a guarantee of receiving our full inheritance. The Greek word for down payment (pledge) is *arrabōn* and is used in Greek culture for "engagement ring."

c 5:9 Or "at home or away from home."

d 5:9 Or "our driving ambition."

e 5:9 Or "in full agreement with him."

f 5:10 Or "judgment seat."

will be duly recompensed for our actions done in life,[a] whether good or worthless.

The Message of Reconciliation

[11]Since we are those who stand in holy awe of the Lord,[b] we make it our passion to persuade others *to turn to him*. We know that our lives are transparent before the God who knows us fully, and I hope that we are also well known to your consciences. [12]Again, we are not taking an opportunity to brag, *but giving you information* that will enable you to be proud of us, and to answer those who esteem outward appearances while overlooking what is in the heart.

[13]If we are out of our minds in a blissful, divine ecstasy,[c] it is for God, but if we are in our right minds, it is for your benefit. [14]For it is Christ's love that fuels our passion and motivates us,[d] because we are absolutely convinced that he has given his life for all of us. This means all died with him, [15]so that those who live[e] should no longer live self-absorbed lives but

---

a 5:10 Or "done in the body" or "time spent in the body." The judgment for our sins fell upon Christ on the cross, and the believer will never be judged for his sins. This judgment (scrutinizing) is for rewards. There will be different levels of reward given to believers after death. For some, there will be no reward, yet they will still be saved. See Romans 14:10–12 and 1 Corinthians 3:10–15.

b 5:11 Although the Greek word *phobos* is usually associated with fear or dread, the classic use of the word is "deepest awe/respect." See 1 John 4:18.

c 5:13 The Greek word *existēmi* means to be outside of one's self in a state of blissful ecstasy and filled with pleasure. It is to come into another state of consciousness of being lost in wonder and amazement.

d 5:14 Paul uses the Greek word *synechō* (syn = together with; echō is where we get our English word *echo*), which is translated as "seize, compel, urge, control, lay hold of, overwhelm, completely dominate." Paul is stating that the motivating passion of his life is Christ's love filling his heart, leaving him no choice but to surrender everything to God. Paul gives us seven empowering motivations by which we are to live our lives: 1) the Holy Spirit—verse 5, 2) faith—verse 7, 3) a joyful confidence that we have new bodies waiting for us in heaven—verse 8, 4) our life's passion to live for Christ—verse 9, 5) the knowledge of our appointment to stand before Christ—verse 10, 6) we stand in holy awe of God—verse 11, 7) Christ's endless love for us—verse 14.

e 5:15 Or "and he died for all so that those who live." The repetitive phrase from verse 14

lives that are poured out for him—the one who died for us and now lives again. [16]So then, from now on, we have a new perspective that refuses to evaluate people merely by their outward appearances. For that's how we once viewed the Anointed One, but no longer do we see him with limited human insight.[a]

[17]Now, if anyone is enfolded into Christ, he has become an entirely new creation. All that is related to the old order has vanished.[b] Behold, everything is fresh and new.[c] [18]And God has made all things new,[d] and reconciled[e] us to himself, and given us the ministry of reconciling others to God. [19]In other words, it was through the Anointed One that God was shepherding the world, not even keeping records of their transgressions,[f] and he has entrusted to us the ministry of opening the door of reconciliation to God.[g] [20]We are ambassadors[h] of the Anointed One who carry the message of Christ to the world, as though God were tenderly pleading[i] with them directly through our lips. So we tenderly plead with you on Christ's behalf, "Turn back to God and be reconciled to him." [21]For God

---

has been enfolded into the verse for the sake of English clarity.

a 5:16 From man's point of view, Christ was a blasphemer and false teacher. Yet when we see him from the eyes of faith, we view him as the pure and holy one, God's Son.

b 5:17 This would include our old identity, our life of sin, the power of Satan, the religious works of trying to please God, our old relationship with the world, and our old mind-sets. We are not reformed or simply refurbished, we are made completely new by our union with Christ and the indwelling of the Holy Spirit.

c 5:17 Or "Behold, a new order has come!"

d 5:18 As translated from the Aramaic and implied in the Greek.

e 5:18 Or "who has restored us to friendship with God."

f 5:19 As translated from the Aramaic. The Greek is "God was reconciling the world to himself, not counting their trespasses against them."

g 5:19 As translated from the Aramaic.

h 5:20 To be ambassadors for Christ means that we are his diplomatic agents of the highest rank sent to represent King Jesus and authorized to speak on his behalf. We are the voice of heaven to the earth, invested with royal power through the name of Jesus and authority of his blood.

i 5:20 Or "begging."

made[a] the only one who did not know sin to become sin for us,[b] so that we *who did not know righteousness* might become the righteousness of God through our union with him.[c]

Six
___

Paul's Ministry

[1]Now, since we are God's coworkers, we beg you not to take God's marvelous grace for granted, *allowing it to have no effect on your lives.*[d] [2]For he says,

> I listened to you at the time of my favor.
> And the day when you needed salvation,
> I came to your aid.[e]

---

a 5:21 The Greek word Paul uses is *poieō*, a verb that, when nominalized, is *poiema* (poem, or poetry). Christ is God's poetic masterpiece who became the glorious sacrifice for sin. Though disturbing to the eyes of man, God saw the work of redemption culminated in the masterful poetry of his Son suspended on a cross to give us heaven's righteousness. Read Isaiah 52:10–53:12.

b 5:21 Or "the sin offering." See Exodus 29:14, Leviticus 4:3, Numbers 8:8, and Ephesians 5:2.

c 5:21 This one verse is perhaps the greatest verse in the New Testament to describe our salvation through the sinless Savior and his substitutionary death on the cross. A wonderful divine exchange took place at the cross. All of our sins were left there, our guilt was removed and forever gone, and we walked away with all of God's righteousness. What bliss is ours! Every believer today possesses the perfect and complete righteousness of Christ. We are seen by the Father as righteous as his Son.

d 6:1 Or "not to receive God's grace in vain."

e 6:2 See Isaiah 49:8.

So can't you see? Now is the time to respond to his favor! Now is the day of salvation! [3]We will not place obstacles[a] in anyone's way that hinder them *from coming to salvation* so that our ministry will not be discredited. [4]Yet, as God's servants, we prove ourselves authentic[b] in every way. *For example*:

We have great endurance[c] in hardships
and in persecutions.
We don't lose courage in a time of stress and calamity.
[5]We've been beaten many times,
imprisoned,
and *found ourselves* in the midst of riots.
We've endured many troubles,[d]
had sleepless nights,
and gone hungry.[e]
[6]*We have proved ourselves* by our lifestyles of purity,
by our spiritual insights,
by our patience,
and by showing kindness,
by the Spirit of holiness
and by our uncritical love for you.[f]
[7]*We commend ourselves to you* by our truthful teachings,[g]
by the power of God *working through us,*
and with the mighty weapons[h] of righteousness—

---

a 6:3 Or "scandals that cause people to stumble."
b 6:4 The Aramaic is "reveals our inner souls."
c 6:4 The Aramaic is "profound hope."
d 6:5 Or "labors." The Aramaic can be translated "tortures."
e 6:5 Or "fastings."
f 6:6 The Aramaic can be translated "love without scheming."
g 6:7 Or "the word of truth (*logos*)."
h 6:7 Or "armor."

a *sword* in one hand and a *shield* in the other.[a]

[8]Amid honor or dishonor,[b]
slander or praise—
even when we are treated as deceivers and imposters—
we remain steadfast and true.
[9]We are unknown nobodies whom everyone knows.
We are frequently at death's door,
yet here we are, still alive!
We have been severely punished
yet not executed.
[10]We may suffer,
yet in every season[c] we are always found rejoicing.
We may be poor,
yet we bestow great riches on many.
We seem to have nothing,
yet in reality we possess all things.[d]

[11]My friends at Corinth, our hearts are wide open to you and we speak freely, holding nothing back from you. [12]If there is a block in our relationship, it is not with us, for we carry you in our hearts with great love, yet you still withhold your affections[e] from us. [13]So I speak to you as our children. Make room in your hearts for us as we have done for you.

---

a 6:7 Or "weapons of righteousness for the right hand and for the left." By implication, this would mean a shield and a sword—every warrior's weapons.

b 6:8 The Aramaic is "cursed (by others)."

c 6:10 As translated by the Aramaic.

d 6:10 What an amazing list of characteristics of true apostolic ministry. These are the virtues that endeared Paul and his ministry companions to the churches and validated his authority as an example to them of God's true servant.

e 6:12 Or "tender mercies." Second Corinthians is Paul's most intimate and descriptive letter. He writes of his inner feelings here more than in any other letter.

The Temple of the Living God

¹⁴Don't continue to team up with unbelievers in mismatched alliances,ᵃ for what partnership is there between righteousness and rebellion? Who could mingle light with darkness? ¹⁵What harmony can there be between Christ and Satan?ᵇ Or what does a believer have in common with an unbeliever? ¹⁶What friendship does God's templeᶜ have with demons?ᵈ For indeed, we are the temple of the living God, just as God has said:

**I will make my home in them and walk among them.
I will be their God, and they will be my people.ᵉ**

¹⁷For this reason,

**"Come out from among them and be separate," says the Lord.
"Touch nothing that is unclean, and I will embrace you.ᶠ
¹⁸I will be a true Father to you,ᵍ
And you will be my beloved sons and daughters,"
says the Lord Yahweh Almighty.ʰ**

---

a 6:14 Paul's teaching here includes marital, business, and personal relationships. We never abandon our responsibility to reach the world (1 Corinthians 5:9–10), but we must steer clear of relationships that will divide our loyalty to Christ.

b 6:15 Or "Belial (the worthless one)," a term for Satan.

c 6:16 The temple in Jerusalem was still standing when Paul wrote this.

d 6:16 As translated from the Aramaic. The Greek is "idols."

e 6:16 See Leviticus 26:12, Jeremiah 32:38, and Ezekiel 37:27.

f 6:17 Or "I will welcome you (within)." See Isaiah 52:11 and Ezekiel 20:41.

g 6:18 God himself will assume the role of caring for us and meeting our needs, giving himself eternally to us. See Psalm 103:18 and Malachi 1:6.

h 6:18 As translated from the Aramaic. See 2 Samuel 7:14 and Isaiah 43:6. Paul is paraphrasing Old Testament texts, changing phases and combining them to make his point. Jesus likewise often paraphrased Old Testament verses as he taught the people.

Seven

Living Holy Lives

¹Beloved ones, with promises like these, and because of our deepest respect and worship of God, we must remove everything from our lives[a] that contaminates body and spirit, and continue to complete the development of holiness within us.

²Again, I urge you, make room for us in your hearts, for we have wronged[b] no one, corrupted[c] no one, and taken advantage[d] of no one. ³I'm not saying this to condemn you, for I already told you that we carry you permanently in our hearts—and you'll stay there throughout our lives, for we will live together and die together. ⁴With an open heart let me freely say how very proud I am of you and how often I boast about you. In fact, *when I think of you* my heart is greatly encouraged and overwhelmed with joy, despite our many troubles.

Paul in Macedonia

⁵Even after we came into the province of Macedonia,[e] we found no relief. We were restless and exhausted; troubles met us at every turn. Outwardly

---

a 7:1 Or "purify ourselves." Believers today must take an active and disciplined approach to spiritual maturity and living holy lives. Grace never removes our responsibility to be faithful to God. Grace empowers us to do what pleases God (Philippians 2:13).

b 7:2 The Aramaic is "We have hated no one."

c 7:2 That is, they had not led people astray from right doctrine. They corrupted no one's *faith*.

d 7:2 Or "We have cheated no one (for financial gain)." These are the three goals every minister should set for his or her calling: 1) to do no wrong to another nor to "hate" anyone, 2) to not corrupt or lead anyone astray, and 3) to never use his or her authority to take advantage of anyone by cheating for personal gain. Paul had a blameless history in ministry.

e 7:5 This was after Paul left Troas and where he wrote his "severe letter" to the Corinthians (2 Corinthians 2:12–13).

I faced conflicts and inwardly emotional turmoil.[a] [6]But God, who always knows how to encourage the depressed, encouraged us greatly by the arrival of Titus. [7]We were relieved not only to see him but because of the report he brought us of how you refreshed his heart. He told us of your affection toward me, your deep remorse, and how concerned you were for me. This truly made my heart leap for joy!

Godly Remorse Over Sin

[8]Even if my letter made you sorrowful, I don't regret sending it (even though I felt awful for a moment when I heard how it grieved you). [9]Now I'm overjoyed—not because I made you sad, but because your grief led you to a deep repentance. You experienced godly sorrow, and as God intended, it brought about gain for you, not loss, so that no harm has been done by us. [10]God designed us to feel remorse over sin in order to produce repentance that leads to victory.[b] This leaves us with no regrets. But the sorrow of the world works death.

[11]Can't you see the good fruit that has come, as God intended, because of your remorse over sin?[c] Now you are eager to do what is

---

a 7:5 Or "fears." The Aramaic is "on the outside battles and on the inside surrendering." With great honesty, Paul discloses his feelings while in Macedonia. He was beset with adversaries who opposed him, problems and arguments within the church, and persecution at every turn. Paul was emotionally torn by all the conflicts among the believers and feared for Titus's safety. He was worried about how the Corinthians would receive his "severe letter," plus there is a hint in his words that his concern was wearing him down both physically and emotionally. Being honest about our emotions is the first step in finding comfort and peace. Paul's example of a leader opening his heart to his people should not be missed by this generation.

b 7:10 Or "deliverance (salvation)."

c 7:11 Both the Hebraic and Greek concepts of repentance are literally "to turn from sin and come back to God"; that is, "to have a change of mind/direction." This involves the "sorrow" or "remorse" of our hearts before God. Repentance is not a sterile, feeling-less act of changing direction. Paul makes it clear that godly remorse is a "God-intended" feeling that moves the heart back to God. Our repentance is not a work of the flesh but the result of God's Spirit stirring our conscience. Peter's godly remorse over his denial of Christ eventually led him to experience a complete inner healing, while Judas's remorse led him to suicide.

right! Look at the indignation you experienced over what happened and how alarmed you became. What holy longing it awakened, what passion *for God*, and how ready you were to bring justice to the offender. Your response has proved that you are free of blame in this matter.

¹²So I wrote you not simply to correct the one who did the wrong or on the behalf of the one who was wronged, but to help you realize in God's sight how loyal you are to us. ¹³Your response leaves us so encouraged! You've made us even more joyful upon hearing of how you refreshed Titus, for his mind was set at ease by all of you. ¹⁴I have not been embarrassed by you, for the things I bragged about you to Titus were not proven false. Just as everything we said to you was true, so our boasting to Titus about you has proven to be true as well. ¹⁵His affection toward you has grown as he remembers your obedience and how warmly you welcomed him with fear and trembling. ¹⁶I'm beside myself with joy! I am so confident in you!

Eight

Generosity of the Churches

¹Beloved ones, we must tell you about the grace God poured out upon the churches of Macedonia. ²For even during a season of severe difficulty and tremendous suffering, they became even more filled with joy. From the depths of their extreme poverty, super-abundant joy overflowed into an act of extravagant generosity. ³For I can verify that they spontaneously gave, not only according to their means but far beyond what they could afford. ⁴They actually begged us for the privilege of sharing in this ministry

of giving to God's holy people *who are living in poverty*. [5]They exceeded our expectations by first dedicating themselves fully to the Lord and then to us, according to God's pleasure.[a] [6]That is why we appealed to Titus, since he was the one who got you started and encouraged you to give, so he could help you complete this generous undertaking on your behalf. [7]You do well and excel in every respect—in unstoppable faith, in powerful preaching, in revelation knowledge, in your passionate devotion, and in sharing the love we have shown to you. So make sure that you also excel in grace-filled generosity.[b]

[8]I'm not saying this as though I were issuing an order but to stir you to greater love by mentioning the enthusiasm *of the Macedonians* as a challenge to you.[c] [9]For you have experienced the extravagant grace of our Lord Jesus Christ, that although he was infinitely rich, he impoverished himself for our sake, so that by his poverty, we could become rich beyond measure.

[10]So here are my thoughts concerning this matter, and it's in your best interests. Since you made such a good start last year, both in the grace of giving and in your longing to give, [11]you should finish what you started.[d] You were so eager in your intentions to give, so go do it. Finish this act of worship according to your ability to give. [12]For if the intention and desire are there, *the size of the gift doesn't matter*. Your gift is fully

---

a 8:5 Under persecution and desperately poor, the churches of Macedonia (Philippi, Thessalonica, and Berea) gave more than just an extravagant offering. They fully surrendered themselves to the Lord and gave out of a longing to fulfill God's pleasure. This is the key to generous giving. First we dedicate our hearts to God, which includes our finances, then we give to God's work as he directs us. Throughout 2 Corinthians, giving is described as a "grace" that God places on our lives, which empowers our generosity.

b 8:7 Notice the features of godliness in this verse that should be seen in our lives and ministries: 1) We excel in everything. 2) We have unstoppable faith. 3) We have an anointing of grace to speak the Word. 4) We have revelation knowledge. 5) We have passionate devotion. 6) We show love. 7) We are generous.

c 8:8 Or "to test your love by the eagerness of others."

d 8:11 Or "Get on with it and finish the job!"

acceptable to God according to what you have, not what you don't have. [13]I'm not saying this in order to ease someone else's load by overloading you, but as a matter of fair balance. [14]Your surplus could meet their need, and their abundance may one day meet your need. This equal sharing of abundance will mean a fair balance.[a] [15]As it is written:

> The one who gathered much didn't have too much,
> and the one who gathered little didn't have too little.[b]

Titus Sent to Corinth

[16]We give thanks to God for putting the same devotion I have for you into the heart of Titus. [17]Of course, he enthusiastically accepted our request to go to Corinth, but because he carries you in his heart, he'd already planned on coming. [18]So we're sending with him the brother[c] who is greatly honored and respected in all the churches for his work of evangelism. [19]Not only that, he has been appointed by the churches to be our traveling companion as we carry and dispense this generous gift that glorifies the Lord and shows how eager we are to help. [20]*We are sending a team* in order to avoid any criticism over how we handle this wonderfully

---

a 8:14 Apparently, the Corinthian church was not poor. They had intended, a year prior to receiving this letter, to make a generous offering to the believers in Jerusalem living in poverty. Paul encourages them to now follow through with their pledge. Note the principles of giving Paul teaches them in verses 10–15: 1) A willing, cheerful offering is more important than the amount. 2) Financial commitments of giving are to be taken seriously. 3) We are to share our substance with those in need, because the time may come when we may need their gifts. 4) Our giving reflects our devotion to Christ. 5) We are to give what we are able and not stress about what we cannot give. We are to give in proportion to our income.

b 8:15 See Exodus 16:18.

c 8:18 This brother and the one mentioned in verse 22 were identified as apostles. Many have tried unsuccessfully to identify whom they might have been. Some of the names considered include Timothy, Luke, Barnabas, Apollos, Mark, Erastus, Silas, Sopater, Aristarchus, Secundus, Gaius, Tychicus, and Trophimus. Regardless of these apostles' identity, we know that Titus was the leader of this delegation and that all three were apostles of the church. See Ephesians 4:11.

generous gift, 21for we intend to do what is right and we are totally open both to the Lord's inspection and to man's. 22So we're sending with them another brother who is faithful and proven to be a man of integrity. He is passionate to help you now more than ever, for he believes in you.

23Concerning the credentials of Titus, he's my partner and coworker in ministry for you. As for the brothers coming with him, they are apostles of the churches, which are the glory of the Anointed One.ᵃ 24So demonstrate to them how much you love, and prove that our boasting of you is justified.

Nine

The Offering for Needy Believers

1Actually, there's no need to write you about this contribution for the holy believers *in Jerusalem,* 2for I already know that you are on board and eager to help.ᵇ I keep boasting to the churches of Macedonia about your passion to give, telling them that the believers of Corinthᶜ have been preparing to give for a year. Your enthusiasm is contagious—it has stirred many of them to do likewise. 3Still, I thought it would be best to send these brothers to receive the offering that you've prepared, so that our

---

a 8:23 Although ambiguous in the Greek text, the clause "which are the glory of the Anointed One" most likely refers to the churches. God's church is his glorious bride on the earth, which brings him glory through all the ages. If referring to Titus and his delegation, this verse would mean that the apostles are the glory of the Anointed One.

b 9:2 The Aramaic is "I know the goodness of your impulses (intentions)." Paul was not hesitant to point out the obvious qualities and virtues of others.

c 9:2 Or "Achaia," the Roman province where Corinth was situated.

boasting about how you were ready to give would not be found hollow.
[4]For if, after boasting of our confidence in you, some of the Macedonians were to come with me and find that you were not prepared, we would be embarrassed—to say nothing of you. [5]That's why I've requested that the brothers come before I do and make arrangements in advance for the substantial offering you pledged. Then it will be seen as a matter of generosity and not under pressure, as something you felt forced to do.

Hilarious Generosity

[6]Here's my point. A stingy sower[a] will reap a meager harvest, but the one who sows from a generous spirit will reap an abundant harvest. [7]Let giving flow from your heart, not from a sense of religious duty. Let it spring up freely from the joy of giving—all because God loves hilarious generosity![b] [8]Yes, God is more than ready to overwhelm you with every form of grace, so that you will have more than enough of everything[c]—every moment and in every way. He will make you overflow with abundance in every good thing you do. [9]Just as the Scriptures say *about the one who trusts in him*:

> **Because he has sown extravagantly and given to the poor,**
> **his kindness and generous deeds will never be forgotten.**[d]

---

a 9:6 The Aramaic is "the one who sows with a storehouse of seed (remaining)." This describes a farmer who is stingy with his sowing. Since he has a storehouse of seed, he can afford to sow liberally.

b 9:7 See Proverbs 22:8 LXX. There are seven things in the Bible that God loves: 1) the resident foreigner or immigrant (Deuteronomy 10:19, 2) righteousness in our affairs with others (Psalm 11:7), 3) justice (Psalm 37:28), 4) the gates of Zion (Psalm 87:2), 5) his righteous people (Psalm 146:8), 6) a hilarious or cheerful giver (2 Corinthians 9:7), and 7) those he disciplines (Hebrews 12:6).

c 9:8 The Greek word Paul uses is *autarkeia*, and it is found in classical Greek as meaning "independently wealthy, needing nothing." See Aristotle. *Pol.* 1. 8, 14.

d 9:9 See Psalm 112:9.

[10]This generous God who supplies abundant seed[a] for the farmer, *which becomes* bread for our meals,[b] is even more extravagant toward you. First he supplies[c] every need, plus more. Then he multiplies the seed *as you sow it,* so that the harvest of your generosity will grow.[d] [11]You will be abundantly enriched in every way as you give generously on every occasion,[e] for when we take your gifts to those in need,[f] it causes many to give thanks to God.

[12]The priestly ministry[g] you are providing through your offering not only supplies what is lacking for God's people, it inspires an outpouring[h] of praises and thanksgiving to God himself. [13]For as your extremely generous offering meets the approval[i] *of those in Jerusalem,* it will cause them to give glory to God—all because of your loyal support and allegiance to the gospel of Christ, as well as your generous-hearted partnership with them toward those in need. [14]Because of this extraordinary grace, which God has lavished on you, they will affectionately remember you in their prayers. [15]Praise God for his astonishing gift, which is far too great for words![j]

---

a 9:10 The Greek word *epichorēgeo* is used in Greek literature for someone who pays all expenses for the drama/choir (production), plus more, providing income for those who take part. God is seen as the Leader of the divine choir, orchestrating everything and providing all that is needed to bring forth the sounds of his glory on the earth.

b 9:10 See Isaiah 55:10.

c 9:10 The Greek word is *chorēgeo* (see previous footnote).

d 9:10 Or "righteousness," used in this context as "generosity (righteous works of benevolence."

e 9:11 Or "You will always be rich enough to be generous at all times."

f 9:11 Or "through us."

g 9:12 The Greek word *leitourgia* (similar to "liturgy") is used in Luke 1:23 for the priestly ministry of Zechariah in the temple.

h 9:12 Or "a super-abounding."

i 9:13 Or "passes the test."

j 9:15 The Greek and Aramaic texts have a clean break at this point. This has caused some scholars to conclude that chapters 10–13 may have originally been separated from the earlier chapters, which could imply that the following four chapters make up the missing letter of Paul to the Corinthians. If this is so, when reading 2 Corinthians, one could begin with Chapters 10–13 (Paul's missing letter), then read from Chapters 1–9. The term for

Ten

Paul's Defense of His Ministry

[1]Now, please listen, for I need to address an issue. I'm making this personal appeal to you by the gentleness[a] and self-forgetfulness of Christ. I am the one who is "humble and timid" when face-to-face with you but "bold and outspoken" when a safe distance away.[b] [2]Now I plead with you that when I come, don't force me to take a hard line with you (which I'm willing to do) by daring to confront[c] those who mistakenly believe that we are living by the standards of the world, *not by the Spirit's wisdom and power.* [3-4]For although we live in the natural realm, we don't wage a military campaign employing human weapons, *using manipulation to achieve our aims.* Instead, our *spiritual* weapons are energized with divine power to effectively dismantle the defenses *behind which people hide.*[d] [5]We can demolish every deceptive fantasy[e] that opposes God and break through every arrogant attitude that is raised up in defiance of the true knowledge of God. We capture, like prisoners of war, every thought[f]

---

this is "appending"; that is, taking an earlier document and adding a later manuscript to it. Yet in this case, the earlier document is appended.

a 10:1 The Aramaic is "peace" or, literally, "by the oasis rest."

b 10:1 Paul is apparently quoting their own words that they used to describe him.

c 10:2 Literally, "Don't force me to be severe with the confidence with which I reckon to dare." Paul pleads with them not to mistake his humility as weakness or an unwillingness to act with authority.

d 10:4 Or "strongholds." The Aramaic word for strongholds can also be translated "rebellious castles." Paul seems to be referring to demonic strongholds or centers of opposition to the light of the gospel.

e 10:5 Or "citadels of argumentations," which include fantasies.

f 10:5 Or "every scheme." Paul is using the concept of taking prisoners of war, but in this case the prisoners held captive are faulty patterns of thought that defy God's authority.

and insist that it bow in obedience to the Anointed One. ⁶*Since we are armed with such dynamic weaponry,* we stand ready to punish[a] any trace of rebellion, as soon as you choose complete obedience.[b]

Paul Responds to Criticism

⁷You seem to always be looking at people by their outward appearances.[c] If someone is confident that he belongs to Christ, he should remind himself of this: we belong to Christ no less than he does. ⁸I am not ashamed, even if I've come across as one who has overstated the authority given to us by the Lord. For it is the authority to help build you up, not tear you down. ⁹I don't want to seem as though I'm trying to bully you with my letters. ¹⁰For I can imagine some of you saying, "His letters are authoritative and stern, but when he's with us, he's not that impressive[d] and he's a poor speaker."[e] ¹¹Such a person should realize that when we arrive, there will be no difference in the actions we take and the words we write.

---

a 10:6 Or "court martial."

b 10:6 This completes one long, complicated Greek sentence that began in verse 3. In this passage Paul describes four arenas of our warfare: 1) We are empowered by grace and with the gospel to dismantle strongholds. 2) We demolish arguments, opinions, theories, and philosophies. 3) We take captive every thought to insist that it become obedient to the mind of Christ. 4) We stand ready and willing to wage war and defeat the enemy (Ephesians 6:10–18).

c 10:7 The Aramaic is "You focus on people's faces."

d 10:10 Or "he's weak."

e 10:10 Greece was known as a land of eloquent speakers. Orators were professionally trained to address crowds. It seems some people were judging Paul by comparing his speaking gift to the eloquent speeches of others. Yet Paul was a brilliant teacher, not a trained orator. True leadership is much more than our speaking ability. Our influence is not limited to a rousing sermon, but we will affect the lives of many if we walk in purity, led by the Holy Spirit. Both Moses and Jeremiah saw themselves as poor speakers. See Exodus 4:10–12 and Jeremiah 1:6.

Paul's Apostolic Mandate

[12]Of course, we wouldn't dare to put ourselves in the same class or compare ourselves with those who rate themselves so highly. They compare themselves to one another[a] and make up their own standards to measure themselves by, and then they judge themselves by their own standards. What self-delusion! [13]But we are those who choose to limit our boasting to only the measure of the work[b] to which God has appointed us—a measure that, by the way, has reached as far as you. [14]And since you are within our assigned limits, we didn't overstep our boundaries of authority by being the first to announce to you the wonderful news of the Anointed One. [15]We're not trying to take credit for the ministry done by others, going beyond the limits *God set for us*. Instead, our hope soars as your faith continues to grow, causing a great expansion of our ministry among you. [16]Then we can go and preach the good news in the regions beyond you without trespassing on the ministry sphere of other laborers and what they have already done. [17]For:

The one who boasts must boast in the Lord.[c]

[18]*So let's be clear.* To have the Lord's approval and commendation is of greater value than bragging about oneself.

---

a 10:12 The Aramaic is "copying one another." God has made each of us unique and given us spiritual gifts that are unique. It is never wise to copy or compare yourself to another believer. Pride will result if we see ourselves as better than someone else, or discouragement if we see ourselves as less valuable than someone else. We don't live by comparison to others but by Christ's life in us.

b 10:13 Or "the sphere of the allocation (given to us)." Paul uses the Greek word *metron*, which was the length of a race course (Greek *dromos*). It was the word used to define the boundaries of a Greek stadium. One could say that Paul stayed within his lane and knew the limits of his measure (*metron*) of spiritual authority.

c 10:17 See Jeremiah 9:24.

Eleven

The Virgin Bride of Christ

[1]Now, please bear with some of my "craziness" for a moment. Yes, please be patient with me.

[2]*You need to know that* God's passion[a] is burning inside me for you, because, like a loving father, I have pledged your hand in marriage to Christ, your true bridegroom. I've also promised that I would present his fiancée to him as a pure virgin bride.[b] [3]But now I'm afraid that just as Eve was deceived by the serpent's clever lies, your thoughts may be corrupted and you may lose your single-hearted devotion and pure love for Christ. [4]For you seem to gladly tolerate anyone[c] who comes to you preaching a pseudo-Jesus, not the Jesus we have preached. You have accepted a spirit and gospel that is false, rather than the Spirit and gospel you once embraced. How tolerant you have become of these imposters!

Super-Apostles?

[5]Now, I believe that I am not inferior in any way to these special "super-apostles"[d] you are attracted to. [6]For although I may not be a polished or eloquent speaker, I'm certainly not an amateur in revelation knowledge. Indeed, we have demonstrated this to you time and again.

---

a 11:2 Or "godly jealousy."

b 11:2 Paul uses the imagery of a bride and bridegroom to describe our relationship to Christ. See Hosea 2:19–20, John 3:29–30, Ephesians 5:25–27, Revelation 19:6–8, and Revelation 21.

c 11:4 Or possibly a reference to "the serpent."

d 11:5 Or "hyper-apostles."

⁷Have I committed a sin by degrading myself to dignify you? Was I wrong to preach the gospel of God to you free of charge?ᵃ ⁸I received ample financial support from other churches just so that I could *freely* serve you. ⁹Remember, when I was with you I didn't bother anyone when I needed money, for my needs were always supplied by my Macedonian friends.ᵇ So I was careful, and will continue to be careful, that I never become a burden to you in any way.

¹⁰As the reality of Christ lives within me, my glad boast *of offering the gospel free of charge* will not be silenced throughout the region of Achaia.ᶜ ¹¹Why? Is it because I have no love for you? God knows how much I love you! ¹²But in order to eliminate the opportunity for those "super-apostles" to boast that their ministry is on the same level as ours I will continue this practice. ¹³For they are not true apostles but deceitfulᵈ ministers who masquerade as "special apostles"ᵉ of the Anointed One. ¹⁴That doesn't surprise us, for even Satan transforms himself to appear as an angel of light!ᶠ ¹⁵So it's no wonder his servants also go about pretending to be ministers of righteousness. But in the end they will be exposed and get exactly what they deserve.

---

a 11:7 Paul received financial support for preaching the gospel and could have asked the Corinthians to support him (Matthew 10:10). But while among them, he refused to receive their gifts and relied on other churches to support him. He did this to set himself apart from the "super-apostles" in Corinth and to demonstrate that his ministry would not be bought.

b 11:9 Or "the brothers." This was most likely from the church of Philippi. See Philippians 4:15–16.

c 11:10 That is, the region where Corinth was located.

d 11:13 Or "dishonest."

e 11:13 Or "who change their form into super-apostles."

f 11:14 In the Jewish pseudepigraphical book, The Apocalypse of Moses, the temptation of Eve is given, and it includes Satan masquerading himself as an angel of light. In the same way, these false apostles were claiming to be sent from Christ but were peddling another gospel.

Paul Speaks as a "Fool"

[16]So I repeat. Let no one think that I'm a fool. But if you do, at least show me the patience you would show a fool, so that I too may boast a little. [17]Of course, what I'm about to tell you is not with the Lord's authority, but as a "fool." [18]For since many love to boast about their worldly achievements,[a] allow me the opportunity to join them. [19]And since you are so smart and so wise to gladly put up with the foolishness of others, *now put up with mine.* [20]You actually allow these imposters to put you into bondage, take complete advantage of you, and rob you blind! How easily you endure those who, in their arrogance, destroy your dignity or even slap you in the face. [21]I must admit, to our shame that we were too "weak" to relate to you the way they do. But now let me dare to boast like a "fool."

Paul Boasts in His Sufferings for Christ

[22]Are these "super-apostles" of yours Hebrews? I am too. Are they Israelites? So am I. Are they descendants of Abraham? Me too! [23]Are they servants of the Anointed One? I'm beside myself when I speak this way, but I am much more of a servant than they. I have worked much harder for God, taken more beatings, and been dragged to more prisons than they. I've been flogged excessively, multiple times, even to the point of death.[b]

[24]Five times I've received thirty-nine lashes from the Jewish leaders.[c] [25]Three times I experienced being beaten with rods.[d] Once they stoned

---

a 11:18 Or "after the flesh (according to earthly distinctions)."

b 11:23 See 1 Corinthians 15:31 and 2 Corinthians 4:11.

c 11:24 Or "forty lashes minus one." Paul received a total of 196 lashings in his lifetime. It was the custom that if anyone was sentenced to lashings, the punishers must ensure that they did not exceed forty, so they only struck the victim thirty-nine times. See Deuteronomy 25:3.

d 11:25 See Acts 16:22–23.

me.[a] Three times I've been shipwrecked;[b] for an entire night and a day I was adrift in the open sea. [26]In my difficult travels I've faced many dangerous situations: perilous rivers, robbers, foreigners, and even my own people. I've survived deadly peril in the city, in the wilderness, with storms at sea, and with spies posing as believers. [27]I've toiled to the point of exhaustion and gone through many sleepless nights. I've frequently been deprived of food and water, left hungry and shivering out in the cold, lacking proper clothing.[c]

[28]And besides these painful circumstances, I have the daily pressure of my responsibility for all the churches, with a deep concern weighing heavily on my heart for their welfare. [29]*I am not aloof*, for who is *desperate and* weak and I do not feel their weakness? Who is led astray into sin and I do not burn with zeal *to restore him*?[d]

[30]If boasting is necessary, I will boast about examples of my weakness. [31]The God and Father of the Lord Jesus, who is eternally praised, knows that I am speaking the truth. [32]Once, when I was in Damascus, the governor[e] under King Aretas[f] had his troops searching for me to have me arrested, [33]but I was stuffed in a basket[g] and lowered down through a window and managed to escape.

---

a 11:25 See Acts 14:19 with footnote.

b 11:25 Since the shipwreck mentioned in Acts 27:39–44 happened after Paul wrote to the Corinthians, his total shipwrecks were four. Apparently the three he mentions here took place during his earlier missionary journeys. Some have calculated that Paul had made eight or nine voyages at the time of this writing.

c 11:27 In verses 23–27 Paul uses his experiences of enduring suffering and hardships as the validation of his apostolic ministry. He would one day sacrifice his life for the gospel while in Rome. In Chapter 12 Paul will use visions and spiritual encounters from God to further validate his role as an apostle of Christ.

d 11:29 Or "ablaze with anger."

e 11:32 Or "ethnarch," a politically appointed leader over a specific ethnic group, who represents the king.

f 11:32 He was the father-in-law of Herod Antipas.

g 11:33 This was a large, braided wicker basket. Humiliated by this ordeal, one could say that Paul was a "basket case."

Twelve

Paul's Visions and Revelations

¹Although it may not accomplish a thing, I need to move on and boast about supernatural visions and revelations of the Lord.[a] ²Someone I'm acquainted with, who is in union with Christ, was swept away fourteen years ago in an ecstatic experience. He was taken into the third heaven,[b] but I'm not sure if he was in his body or out of his body—only God knows. ³And I know that this man[c] (again, I'm not sure if he was still in his body or taken out of his body—God knows) ⁴was caught up in an ecstatic experience and brought into paradise,[d] where he overheard many wondrous

---

a 12:1 Or "from the Lord."

b 12:2 Although there are Jewish traditions that present a cosmology of seven levels of heaven, most scholars conclude that the third heaven is the highest realm of the immediate presence of God.

c 12:3 There a number of compelling reasons to conclude that the "man" Paul refers to is himself. 1) He knew the exact time this ecstatic experience took place. 2) He knew that what was overheard in the third heaven was "inexpressible" and not to be repeated. 3) He was not certain about what state he was is in (embodied/disembodied). 4) In verse 7 he uses the first-person pronoun *I* ("I was given a thorn in the flesh") as a counterbalance to the high level of revelation that Paul had received. It was a common literary device, a rhetorical ploy, to avoid speaking of oneself directly in this fashion and by using the phrase, "I am acquainted with a man," when he, in fact, was referring to himself. It is a sign of Paul's humility and integrity that he did not "boast" of this event that took place fourteen years earlier. Many today who have experiences with God are quick to tell what happened. Paul veiled his heavenly encounters with God and waited to share them only when it was appropriate and faith-building for others. Not every experience we have is meant to be shared immediately. This is what got Joseph the dreamer thrown into a pit by his jealous brothers.

d 12:4 What Paul described as the third heaven in verse 3 is now called Paradise. It is possible that Paul is recounting two different experiences, or possibly one experience in which he ascended into two levels or two realms of encounter (third heaven and then Paradise/seventh heaven). The third possibility is that it was one and the same place, described with different terms. For more on the term *paradise* (Hebrew *pardes*, Aramaic *pardesa*, Greek *paradeisos*), see Genesis 2:9, Luke 23:43, and Revelation 2:7.

and inexpressible secrets[a] *that were so sacred* that no mortal is permitted to repeat them.[b] [5]I'm ready to boast of such an experience, but for my own good I refuse to boast unless it concerns my weaknesses.[c] [6]However, if I were to boast, it wouldn't be ridiculous at all, for I would be speaking the truth. Yet I will refrain, lest others think higher of me than what I demonstrate with my life and teaching.

Paul's "Thorn"

[7]The extraordinary level of the revelations I've received is no reason for anyone to exalt me.[d] For this is why a thorn in my flesh was given to me, the Adversary's messenger sent to harass me,[e] keeping me from becoming arrogant. [8]Three times I pleaded with the Lord to relieve me of this. [9]But he answered me, "My grace is always more than enough for you,[f] and my power finds its full expression through your weakness." So I will celebrate my weaknesses, for when I'm weak I sense more deeply the mighty power of Christ living in me.[g] [10]So I'm *not defeated* by my weakness, but delighted! For when I feel my weakness and endure

---

a 12:4 Or "words" or "matters" or "things." Paul was privileged to see and hear of mysteries that are beyond the reach of human language and unable to be spoken by human lips.

b 12:4 See also Revelation 10:4.

c 12:5 The Aramaic is "afflictions."

d 12:7 The true character of spiritual revelations is that they exalt Christ, not people. It is a paradox that the greater our understanding of God we receive, the less we truly know and the more humble we become. Paul refused to be exalted in the eyes of others. This is the nature of true apostolic ministry.

e 12:7 Or "to slap my face" or "to box my ears." Paul did not have a demon, though it was possible that a demon followed him to harass and hinder. This is more likely a metaphor of the harassment he endured, the constant misunderstanding and persecution that came to him because of his faith in Jesus. There is no indication that this "thorn" was a sickness. In Paul's list of hardships (2 Corinthians 11:23–27) he does not mention a sickness or disease.

f 12:9 Or "My grace is continuously sufficient in you (to ward it off)."

g 12:9 Or "The power of Christ rests upon me like a tent or tabernacle (providing me shelter)."

mistreatment—when I'm surrounded with troubles on every side and face persecution *because of my love* for Christ—I am made yet stronger. For my weakness becomes a portal to God's power.

The Signs of an Apostle

11I have become foolish *to boast like this*, but you have forced me to do it, when you should have boasted in me instead. For there is nothing I lack compared to these "super-apostles" of yours, even though I am nothing. 12The things that distinguish a true apostle were performed among you with great perseverance—supernatural signs, startling wonders, and awesome miracles.

13Furthermore, how were you treated worse than the other churches, except that I didn't burden you financially—forgive me for depriving you!*a* 14And now here I am, ready to come to you for the third time,*b* and I still refuse to be a burden to you. For what I really want is your hearts, not your money. After all, children should not have to accumulate resources for their parents, but parents do this for their children. 15*And as a spiritual father to you,* I will gladly spend all that I have and all that I am for you!*c* If I love you more, will you respond by loving me less?*d*

---

a 12:13 Paul appears to be addressing a complaint that he had treated the Corinthians differently than the other churches when, in fact, he had refused their financial support and was helped instead by the Philippians, who aided him financially while in Corinth, and for this he should have been commended by them. The four marks of Paul being a true apostle are: 1) supernatural signs attesting to God's presence and authority, 2) wonderful deeds that could be explained only by a supernatural God, 3) powerful miracles that point to Christ, 4) treating the churches with respect and not wanting to burden them if at all possible, and 5) becoming a true spiritual father to the churches (see verse 15).

b 12:14 It was during Paul's third visit to Corinth that he wrote the letter to the Romans.

c 12:15 Or "for your souls."

d 12:15 Some manuscripts indicate that this is not a rhetorical clause but make it into a concessive clause subordinate to the first half of the verse, effectively changing the meaning to "I will gladly spend all that I am for you, even though you love me less for doing so." Sacrificial love is always the key to opening the hearts of people we minister to and serve.

¹⁶Be that as it may, I haven't been a burden to you at all, yet you say of me, "He's a scoundrel and a trickster!" ¹⁷*But let me ask you this.* Did I somehow cheat or trick you through any of the men I sent your way? ¹⁸I was the one who insisted that Titus and our brother come *and help you.* Did Titus take advantage of you? Didn't we all come to you in the same spirit, *following in the ways of integrity?*

¹⁹I hope that you don't assume that all this time we have simply been justifying ourselves in your eyes? Beloved ones, we have been speaking to you in the sight of God as those joined to Christ, and everything we do is meant to build you up and make you stronger in your faith. ²⁰Now I'm afraid that when I come to you I may find you different than I desire you to be, and you may find me different than you would like me to be. I don't want to find you in disunity, with jealousy and angry outbursts, with selfish ambition, slander, gossip, arrogance, and turmoil. ²¹I'm actually afraid that on my next visit my God will humble me in front of you as I shed tears over those who keep sinning without repenting of their impurity, sexual immorality, and perversion.

Weakness and God's Power

¹This will be my third trip to you. And I will make sure that by the testimony of two or three witnesses every matter will be confirmed.ᵃ ²⁻³Since you are demanding proof that the Anointed One is speaking through me, *I will give*

---

a 13:1 See Deuteronomy 19:15, Matthew 18:16, and 1 Timothy 5:19.

you proof by exercising discipline among you. For just as I told you the last time I was there—and now, though absent, I say it again—that when I come I will not go easy on those whom I've already warned and those who continue to persist in their sin. Christ is not weak or feeble in his dealings with you but mighty and powerful within you. ⁴For although he was crucified as a "weakling," now he lives *robed* with God's power. And we also are "weak ones" *in our co-crucifixion* with him, but now we live in God's triumphant power together with him, which is demonstrated on your behalf.

⁵Now your souls will be strengthened and healed if you hold steadfast to your faith.ᵃ Haven't you already experienced Jesus Christ himself living in you? If not, you are deficient.ᵇ ⁶I hope you understand that we cannot be devalued.ᶜ ⁷But we pray to God that you will be flawless,ᵈ not to validate our ministry among you but so that you may continue on the path of righteousness even if we are denigrated.ᵉ ⁸For in reality, the power we have is used in support of the truth, not against it. ⁹And we claim before Godᶠ that you will be fully equipped and mature, for it brings us great joy when you are strong, even if we seem weak and denigrated.

Paul's Farewell

¹⁰I'm writing my honest feelings to you from afar so that when I arrive I won't have to correct you by using the authority the Lord has given me, for I want to build you up and not tear you down.

---

a 13:5 As translated from the Aramaic. The Greek is "Examine yourselves to see if you are indeed in the faith."

b 13:5 As translated from the Aramaic. The Greek is "unless you are disqualified."

c 13:6 As translated from the Aramaic. The Greek is "You know that we are not disqualified."

d 13:7 See Song of Songs 4:7.

e 13:7 As translated from the Aramaic. The Greek is "even if we appear as disapproved."

f 13:9 The Greek word *eukhomai* (accusative and infinitive construction) means more than prayer; it is to make a claim before God in prayer. The verb is *eukhe,* which means a votive obligation and is translated "make a vow" in Acts 18:18.

[11]Finally, beloved friends,[a] be cheerful! Repair whatever is broken among you, as your hearts are being knit together in perfect unity. Live continually in peace, and God, the source of love and peace, will mingle with you. [12]Greet and embrace one another with the sacred kiss.[b] [13]All of God's holy people send their greetings.

[14]Now, may the grace and joyous favor of the Lord Jesus Christ, the unambiguous love of God, and the precious communion that we share in the Holy Spirit be yours continually. Amen![c]

---

a 13:11 Or "brothers (and sisters)."

b 13:12 What makes a kiss holy or sacred is that it comes from the love of God. See Song of Songs 1:2 and Romans 16:16.

c 13:14 The Aramaic ends with this concluding statement: "The end of the second letter to the Corinthians that was written from Philippi of Macedonia and sent by the hand of Titus."

About the Translator

Dr. Brian Simmons is known as a passionate lover of God. After a dramatic conversion to Christ, Brian knew that God was calling him to go to the unreached people of the world and present the gospel of God's grace to all who would listen. With his wife Candice and their three children, he spent nearly eight years in the tropical rain forest of the Darien Province of Panama as a church planter, translator, and consultant. Brian was involved in the Paya-Kuna New Testament translation project. He studied linguistics and Bible translation principles with New Tribes Mission. After their ministry in the jungle, Brian was instrumental in planting a thriving church in New England (U.S.), and now travels full time as a speaker and Bible teacher. He has been happily married to Candice for over forty-two years and is known to boast regularly of his children and grandchildren. Brian and Candice may be contacted at:

Facebook.com/passiontranslation
Twitter.com/tPtBible

For more information about other books available from The Passion Translation or any of Brian's other books, please visit:

thePassionTranslation.com
StairwayMinistries.org

Notes

Notes

Notes

Notes

thePassionTranslation.com